The Sages Speak About
Immortality

THE *Mananam* SERIES

(*Mananam*–Sanskrit for "Reflection upon the Truth")

(continued on inside back page)

Other Chinmaya Publication Series:

THE *Self-Discovery* SERIES

THE *Hindu Culture* SERIES

T H E *Mananam* S E R I E S

The Sages Speak About
*I*mmortality

CHINMAYA PUBLICATIONS

Chinmaya Publications
Main Office
P.O. Box 129
Piercy, CA 95587, USA

Chinmaya Publications
Distribution Office
560 Bridgetown Pike
Langhorne, PA 19053, USA

Central Chinmaya Mission Trust
Sandeepany Sadhanalaya
Saki Vihar Road
Bombay, India 400 072

Credits:

Series Editors: Margaret Leuverink and Br. Rajeshwar
Front cover and text photographs: Simon Dalrymple
Photograph of Meher Baba: Courtesy of Sheriar Press
Photograph of Eknath Easwaran: Courtesy of Nilgiri Press

Library of Congress Catalog Card Number 95-68108

ISBN 1-880687-08-9

Contents

PART THREE

THE GOAL OF LIFE

Preface

Immortality is not a state of existence to anticipate after the death of the physical body; it is a state of being that is with us even now. To awaken to this essence in ourselves is the goal of human life. Our attitudes and vision of life change completely even when we dimly begin to perceive this state. We discover that this reality is not confined to ourselves alone but is the basis of the entire universe of things and beings. Whereas before we may have felt ourselves to be separate, isolated individuals, we are now aware of our oneness with all. And we become the kind of human being we were meant to be, joyfully participating in life and flowing with love as we can no longer exclude anyone or anything.

This exalted state has been glorified by saints and sages throughout the centuries. Jesus said that we must lose our life in order to gain it. The life to be gained is the life of the Spirit—everlasting, eternal, and immortal. The life we are meant to lose is the little life, limited and full of selfish concerns. Strongly anchored in the Spirit, we become fearless, no longer seeing another, only the One—indestructible, invincible, the Light of lights.

Because the concept of immortality is often associated with the state after the death of the physical body, this book begins with a discussion on "Life After Death." Through the ancient fable of the caterpillar, Yogi Ramacharaka of the Yoga Foundation indicates that death is a change and not an end. He also emphasizes that the argument of the materialists, that everything dies, is untenable to a person with spiritual discernment; one who has made the search inward knows that nothing really dies but only appears to do so. In the next article, Ganga Prasad Upadhyaya of the Arya Samaj writes that people have doubts about the afterlife and reincarnation only because they do not know the classification and functioning of the three bodies. Using everyday examples, he proceeds to explain each of these. He says the balance of mental impressions created by all our intentions, thoughts, and actions defines the subtlest of bodies within us, the causal, which determines our continuance. This is confirmed in the next article by a former President of the Theosophical Society, James Perkins, as he describes his own near-death experience. He recognized that in order to stay in the wondrous region of the universe of light one needs to "have awakened and unfolded one's consciousness to cosmic proportions." Therefore, he stresses the importance of working through all our relationships in "this school of life."

The Vedantic Master Swami Chinmayananda discusses the different qualities or moods of the mind (*gunas*) in the next article. These *gunas* are known as *sattva* (pure), *rajas* (agitated), and *tamas* (inertia). He shows how the most predominant *guna* determines the quality of our thoughts, and thus the direction of the subtle body after death.

Depending on our religious background we all have different ideas of heaven, hell, and purgatory. Part Two, "Concepts of Heaven and Hell," begins with the writings of Leslie D. Weatherhead, who was a Methodist minister in England. He writes that Jesus' teachings could never have contained the idea of eternal punishment. He says if there is such a thing as eternal damnation, it would be valueless. Futhermore, the Lord used the imagery of fire to point out the benefits of the purifying process on a person's character.

The Sufi Master Meher Baba then gives a lucid description of heaven and hell, explaining that they are simply states of mind resulting from experiences acquired through many embodiments.

Grosser desires cause greater suffering after the physical body dies, since they no longer have a medium for expression and fulfillment.

Through the story of a visit to hell and heaven, Swami Chinmayananda points out that when we are selfish, we are in hell and when selfless, in heaven. Commenting on some of the verses from the *Praśna Upaniṣad*, Swami Chinmayananda admonishes us not to waste our life in the mere performance of rituals. He says attainment of the Highest is reserved only for those who have accompanied their noble and charitable acts with dynamic living and meditation upon the ultimate Truth.

From the highest viewpoint it is clear that ideas of heaven, hell, and an immortal soul are created by the mind as part of its self-preservation instinct. These concepts are but stepping stones to take us out of our deeply rooted identification with the body. The ultimate step, of course, is to go beyond any concept of an existent individuality, whether finite or immortal. Some of the means to achieve that awakening are discussed in the next two sections.

Part Three, "The Goal of Life," shows how egocentric desires are responsible for our sense of limitation and reveals the methods for freeing ourselves from them. Swami Tyagananda of the Ramakrishna Mission and editor of the *Vedanta Kesari* states clearly that only when we become desireless can we be truly happy. He uses the allegory of the hawk holding onto a fish and then being chased by other birds. When the hawk drops the fish, the other birds leave him in peace. In the next article, Swami Chinmayananda says that if all Hindu Masters glorify the state of desirelessness, it is due to the fact that all earthly pleasures pale in comparison to the happiness, peace, and harmony experienced by one who has reached this state.

In a dialogue with a seeker, the contemporary sage Nisargadatta Maharaj, reassures us that all blessings will flow automatically when we continue to broaden our awareness of ourselves. The Sufi Master Hazrat Inayat Khan then reiterates that spiritual practices are nothing but processes of playing. The play begins with de-identification from the little "I" and identification with the larger "Thou."

The theme of self-expansion is taken up in the final part, "Toward Eternal Life." Haridas Chaudhuri, a lifelong student of Sri Aurobindo and the late founder and president of the California Institute of Integral Studies, begins this section. He shows how the longing for immortality takes on different expressions in our lives, such as social, idealistic, and personal, depending on the personality of the individual. He also helps clarify the state of immortality, emphasizing that the personality is not liquidated but illumined. "Emancipated from the fetters of egocentricity it becomes cosmocentric." Then the body can function as an effective instrument for expressing the Divine.

In the final article, Eknath Easwaran, founder of the Blue Mountain Center of Meditation, writes that it is not the extinction of the personality that we are striving for, but rather its perfection, by living for the happiness and welfare of all. By defying the condition of pleasure within ourselves and choosing to identify with the changeless, eternal Self, we gain immortality here and now, creating a heaven on earth for ourselves and others.

M.L.

PART ONE

Life After Death

Every body *dies*
but nobody *dies*.

Swami Chinmayananda

The consciousness of the dying person finds itself suddenly relieved of the weight of the body, of the necessity to breathe, and of any physical pain. A sense of soaring through a tunnel of very peaceful, hazy, dim light is experienced by the soul. Then the soul drifts into a state of oblivious sleep, a million times deeper and more enjoyable than the deepest sleep experienced in the physical body. . . . The after-death state is variously experienced by different people in accordance with their modes of living while on earth. Just as different people vary in the duration and depth of their sleep, so do they vary in their experiences after death. The good man who works hard in the factory of life goes into a deep, unconscious, restful sleep for a short while. He then awakens in some region of life in the astral world: "In my Father's house are many mansions." (John 14:2)

Paramahansa Yogananda
Where There is Light

How does the soul find his own place in the astral world? In the astral world, there are no policemen to tell you where you belong, to guide you to the place where you will have to stay. How then does the soul find his own place? When the soul dwells within the physical body, while on earth, it acquires certain vibrations. Each soul vibrates to its own frequency, depending upon the degree of his unselfishness, love and compassion, and purity and prayerfulness. The more unselfish a soul, the more pure and prayerful he is, the greater the frequency of his vibration. When the soul is separated from the body, it goes straight to that part of the astral world that has the same vibrations as that of the migrating soul. Thus, each soul finds his own place in the astral world.

J.P. Vaswani
Life After Death

I

Death:
The Great Illusion

by Yogi Ramacharaka

The human race has been hypnotized with the idea of death, and the common usage of the term reflects the illusion. Those who should know better speak of a person being "cut down by the grim reaper," "cut off in his prime," "his activities terminated," "a busy life brought to an end," and so on. The ideas expressed imply that the individual has been wiped out of existence and reduced to nothingness. Although the major religions teach the joys of the "hereafter" in such strong terms that it seems every believer would welcome the transition, we see that just the opposite takes place. One would think that relatives and friends would wear bright clothes and deck themselves with flowers in celebration of the passage of a loved one to happier and brighter spheres of existence. The average person, however, in spite of his faith and creed, seems to dread the approach of death, and his friends appear in black clothes and give every outward sign of having lost the beloved one forever. In spite of their beliefs, or expression of belief, death has a terror that they seemingly cannot overcome.

To those who have acquired a sense of the illusion of death these frightful emotions have faded away. While they naturally feel the sorrow of temporary separation and the loss of companionship, the loved one is seen to have simply passed on to another phase of life, and nothing has been lost—nothing has perished.

There is a centuries' old Hindu fable about a caterpillar, who feeling the approach of the languor that meant the end of the crawling stage of existence and the beginning of the long sleep of the chrysalis stage, called his friends around him. "It is sad," he said, "to think that I must abandon my life, filled with so many bright promises of future achievement. Cut off in my very prime, I am an example of the heartlessness of nature. Farewell, good friends, farewell forever. Tomorrow I shall be no more."

And, accompanied by the tears and lamentations of his friends, who surrounded him as he lay on his deathbed, he passed away. An old caterpillar remarked sadly: "Our brother has left us. His fate is also ours. One by one we shall be cut down by the scythe of the destroyer, just like grass of the field. By faith we hope to rise again, but perhaps this is but the voice inspired by a vain hope. None of us knows anything positively of another life. Let us mourn the common fate of our race." And they all departed sadly.

The irony of this little fable is clearly perceived by all of us. And we smile at the thought of the ignorance that attended the first stage of transformation of the lowly crawling thing into a glorious-hued creature, which in time will emerge from the sleep of death into a higher form of life. But, smile not, friends, at the illusion of the caterpillar—they were even as you and me. For the Hindu storyteller has pictured human ignorance and illusion in this little fable of the lower forms of life.

Changes of Forms

All occultists recognize in the transformation stages of the caterpillar-chrysalis-butterfly a picture of the transformation that awaits every mortal man and woman. For death to the human being is no more a termination or cessation than the death-sleep of the caterpillar. In either case life does not cease for even a single instant—life persists while nature works her changes. We advise every student to carry with him the lesson of this little fable, told long ago to the children of the Hindu race, and passed on from generation to generation.

Strictly speaking, there is no such thing as death. The name is a lie. The very idea is an illusion growing from ignorance. There is no death—there is nothing but life. Life has many phases and forms, and some phases are called "death" by ignorant people. Nothing really dies—though everything experiences a change of form and activity. As Edwin Arnold so beautifully expressed it in his translation of the *Bhagavad Gītā*:

> Never the spirit was born;
> The spirit shall cease to be never.
> Never was time it was not;
> End and beginning are dreams.
>
> Birthless, deathless, and changeless,
> Remaineth the spirit forever;
> Death hath not touched it at all,
> Dead though the house of it seems.

Materialists frequently urge, as an argument against the persistence of life beyond the stage of death, the assumed fact that everything in nature suffers death, dissolution, and destruction. If such were the case, then it would indeed be reasonable to argue the death of the soul as a logical conclusion. But, in truth, nothing of this kind happens in nature. *Nothing really dies.* What is called death, even of the smallest and apparently most inanimate thing, is merely a change of form and condition of the energy and activities which constitute it. Even the body does not *die*, in the strict sense of the word. The body is not an entity, for it is merely an aggregation of cells, and these cells are merely material vehicles for a certain form of energy which animates and vitalizes them. When the soul passes from the body, the units composing the body manifest repulsion for each other in place of the attraction which formerly held them together. The unifying force which has held them together withdraws its power, and the reverse activity is manifested. As a writer has well said: "The body is never more alive, when it is dead." As another writer has said: "Death is but an aspect of life, and the destruction of one material form is but a prelude to the building up of another." So the argument of the materialists really lack its major premise, and all reasoning based thereon must lead to a false conclusion.

But the advanced occultist, or other spiritually developed person, does not consider the argument of the materialists seriously. Nor would he, even if these arguments were a hundred times more logical. For such a person has awakened within himself the higher psychic and spiritual faculties by which he may actually *know* that the soul does not perish when the body dissolves. When one is able to leave the physical body behind, and actually travel in the regions of the other side, as in the case of many advanced individuals, any speculative discussions or arguments on the reality of life after death take on the appearance of absurdity and futility.

The Song of the Soul

If an individual, who has not yet reached the stage of psychic and spiritual discernment whereby he is given the higher evidence on the question of the survival of the soul, finds his reason demanding something akin to proof, let him turn his mental gaze inward instead of outward. There he will find that which he seeks. For all philosophy teaches us that the world of the inner is far more real than the world of the outer phenomena. In fact, man has no actual knowledge of the outer—all he has is the report of the inner upon the impressions received from the outer. Man sees not the tree at which he is gazing—he perceives but the inverted image of that tree pictured upon his retina. His mind does not even see this image, for it receives only the vibratory report of the nerves whose ends have been excited by that image. So we need not be ashamed of taking mental stock of the inner recesses of our mind, for many of the deepest truths are recorded there.

In the great subconscious and super-conscious regions of the mind, a knowledge of many fundamental truths of the universe are to be found. Two of these greatest truths are: (1) The certainty of the existence of a supreme universal Power supporting the phenomenal world; (2) the certainty of the immortality of the real Self—that something within which fire cannot destroy, water cannot drown, nor air blow away. The mental eye turned inward will always find the "I," with the certainty of its imperishability. It is true that this is a different kind of proof from that required regarding material and physical objects, but what of that? The truth sought is a fact of spiritual inner life, and not of the physical outer life. Therefore, it must be looked for *within*, and not without, the soul itself. The objective intellect concerns physical objects alone. The subjective intellect, or intuition, concerns psychic and spiritual objects. The one is the body of things, the other the soul of things. Look for knowledge, concerning either class of things in its own appropriate region of your being.

Let the soul speak for itself, and you will find that its song will ring forth clearly, strongly, and gloriously. "There is no death, there is no death, there is nothing but life, and that life is Life Everlasting!" This is the song of the soul. Listen, for it is the Silence, for there alone can its vibrations reach your eager ears. It is the Song of Life ever denying death. There is no death—there is nothing but Life Everlasting, forever, and forever, and forever.

II

The Nature of
Our Bodies

by Ganga Prasad Upadhyaya

Those who raise doubts about life after death, are mostly those who have not understood the existence or functioning of the three bodies. It is not difficult to understand them. We use these bodies every day. They are always functioning. But we do not care to know the distinction between one body and another. Some people will ask, "How is it that we do not remember anything of our past lives? Of what use is reincarnation in the development of ourselves if we do not know of what karmas or actions our present life is a reward of? How do we pass from one body to another at the time of death? How long does it take to pass from one body to another? What is the abode and condition of the soul in the interval?" There are several thinkers who have been convinced of the reasonableness of the doctrine of reincarnation. But the above-mentioned doubts obstruct their way. This is because they do not know the tripartite classification of our bodies.

The gross body is visible to all. Eyes, ears, mouth, hands, and feet all form the gross body. It is the subject of physiology and anatomy. The medical doctor understands it in all its details. Others, too, know something about the body. But the limitations of the functions of this body are not known to many. Let us take a concrete example. I have a table before me. I see it. What does it mean? Through light the shape and color of the picture come to the retina and make an impression there. Yet the eye does not retain the picture. It passes it on to the inner something, this something is not the flesh, bone, or blood behind the retina. Nor is it the nerves. From our skin down to the nerves they are all the parts of our gross body. Physiology goes only so far, and not further.

The Subtle and Causal Bodies

If you anatomize the eye or any part of the body, you will not be able to see this picture. But where has this picture gone? When we dream and sleep this picture comes before us. At that time the eye is absolutely at rest. Who sees this picture then? Not the eyes. What was the storehouse where this picture and thousands of others of similar type were treasured? We can say that we see it in dreams with our mental eyes. But this is the metaphorical use. This is no answer. Here is the proof of the existence of the subtle body. The gross body passes all impressions to the subtle body. There they remain safe.

Again, when we see a scene we feel pleasure or pain. This pleasure or pain is not the function of any part of the gross body. The gross body may pull up the cord of the pleasure or pain. But this does not exist there. It is the subtle body through which we feel pleasure or pain. When our gross body is unable to pull up this cord, even the cutting of the parts of the body is not accompanied by pleasure or pain (for example under chloroform).

This subtle body is material in its origin. It is a body. But its stuff is much finer, quite beyond the scope of physical examination. Dreams are a function of this body. So is knowledge. We see that if two tables are put along with two other tables, they make four. Our gross eyes have enabled us to see the chairs, but they did not tell us that they are four in number, or that two and two make four. This was the work of the subtle body.

Go further. When we are in sound sleep, this subtle body

also ceases to function. We are enjoying rest. We neither see the outer world, nor are we seeing dreams. We do not even desire or dislike anything. Still, we are not inactive. We do feel something much finer, finer than ordinary feelings of pain and pleasure, finer than the feeling of desire or hatred, finer than the feeling of any objective knowledge. This feeling leaves its footprints on us. When the sound sleep is over we wake up, and we say that we enjoyed sleep. We are better now than we were when we went to sleep. Sound slumber is not wakefulness. Wakefulness is not sound slumber. But the condition of the sound slumber has left its impression on our wakefulness. That is the aftereffect. This has been said to be the function of our causal body. Our memories do not reside in this causal body, but the quintessence of those memories, call them instincts or tendencies. Our gross body contacted gross objects and took their pictures or impressions. But it did not keep those impressions. It passed them on to the subtle body. There the grossness of the objects disappeared.

A two-mile long road seen while awake appeared two miles long in the dream also. But the grossness of the two miles was not there. There is not so much space in our mind. It cannot contain a two-mile long road. But now this subtle body in its turn does not pass all the sensations it receives to the causal body. It squeezes them out, draws their extracts in the form of tendencies or instincts. The grossness of the sensations is gone. The details of memory are absent. The extracts in the form of instincts are there. This is the action of the causal body. Remember this causal body when you think of death or reincarnation. It is very important. Underline it well. You will need it in further investigation.

The Goal and the Processes

Every action we perform has some goal. To reach that goal a long line of actions is necessary. This we call processes. When the goal is reached, these processes are left out. For instance, we purchase biscuits in the market. The shopkeeper wraps them in a package. The package is the outer covering. The goal is putting these biscuits into our mouth. All else is a process. When the biscuit is put into our mouth, the package becomes useless, and we throw it away.

Go further. The goal of eating biscuits is the production of energy in the body. Chewing, digesting, and other actions are processes. Just as the box was a covering for the biscuits, similarly, biscuits are a covering for the energy. You brought the biscuits in a packet, so that the biscuits may not be spoiled. Energy is enshrined in the biscuits so that it may not be spoiled. The goal is energy, not the biscuits. They are the processes. When the energy is obtained, the rest of the biscuits are thrown away. Our body eliminates the refuse; this is the physical limit of the question.

Go further. We acquire knowledge through observation or study. This knowledge comes to us packed up in bundles of events—which are like the outer coverings of the boxes of the biscuits. The coverings were not our goal. They were mere processes—necessary as processes but not after the goal is reached. Particular events lead to generalization. We squeeze these particular events and draw the quintessence out of them. We forget the details. They are the outer coverings. They should be thrown away as soon as they have done their work.

Just follow the journey that a student of mathematics covers from the day he learned numeration and notation up to the day he becomes a full-fledged mathematician. Think what he has learned, but also calculate how much he has forgotten. Does he remember today those very details of the processes through which the primary teacher taught him the simple addition rule of three plus three? Does he know the details of the sums he solved? Was it necessary to remember those details? Was it possible? Did those details not become actual refuse after a certain stage, worth being thrown away, forgotten? Now he has acquired mathematical instincts, light essence in the form of formulae. Other things were mere processes, too gross to carry. The things of ultimate value are these formulae and not that of the sums that led to these.

Collecting new events is the function of our gross body. To make them rarefied and keep them in finer forms is the function of our subtle and causal bodies. The latter cannot bear the load of grosser objects. They extract the essence.

Take another allegory. You earn money, penny after penny. When you have 240 pennies, you convert them into a pound. Why? One pound is lighter to carry than 240 pennies and yet it has the same value, and whenever necessary, it can bring 240 fresh pennies. You need not carry the burden. Similarly, the rarefied formulae as experiences have ultimate value. They can be applicable to fresher events. These events—a long list of them— must be forgotten to make space in your mind for other formulae. If your pocket is full of copper pennies, it will not be able to hold more coins, therefore, you must change them into lighter pounds. The same holds true in the case of knowledge. We begin with a series of events and isolated objects. We received them respectfully and in wonder. We collect them, sort them, classify them, and generalize them. And as soon as we have boiled them and drawn their extract in the form of generalization, we throw them away as useless refuse.

Ask a master of literature, how much he has forgotten? He had to read many books, page after page, with patience and perseverance, underlining important words, copying out necessary material, cramming a good deal. But does he remember them all? How much has he not forgotten? Take the percentage. But is he poorer for that forgetfulness? If he refused to forget all that and tried to carry all "the load of learning lumbering in his head," he would not have been called learned. Learning does not mean those collections of words, phrases, sentences, or even language. Language also, in the end, comes under the category of processes and not under the goal. The real goal is the experience rarefied in the form of instincts enshrined in our causal body, and they are the only thing that matters. All else is refuse to be thrown away at different stages after their utility is over.

Remember also, by the way, that different substances yield different extracts. The extract of sugarcane is sweet and the extract of chilies is pungent. Good actions make good instincts, and bad actions bad instincts. A series of robberies makes a person a thief, and creates undesirable instincts in him. A series of noble acts makes a person noble and creates quite different instincts in him. As different individuals pass through different environments and diversified experiences their causal bodies are also different.

But one thing should be remembered. It is not easy to read causal bodies. They are so deep. It is difficult to dive down. The gross bodies are easily seen. But their outer appearance is often misleading. For example, a well-dressed butcher and a similarly dressed philanthropist do not appear so different as their causal bodies. Poison and nectar can both be in identically beautiful decanters. Cases can hold gold and iron rings alike. What really matters is the content and not the container, therefore, the importance of causal bodies over gross bodies.

One thing more should be made clear. Our gross bodies change very rapidly. Not so our subtle bodies. Still less our causal bodies. Just as we change our coats often, but not our skins. Similarly our skins, our flesh, our blood undergoes rapid changes. Our habits cling to us firmer than our teeth or our eyes. And our instincts are more durable than our habits.

We Make Our Destinies

It is a well-known saying that we make our own destinies, but what does this sentence mean? What are destinies? And how do we make them? After having read the last few pages, it should be clear as to what is the destiny.

If a person has been earning money and saving it penny after penny, the treasure that he has at the end is his destiny. If a student has been acquiring knowledge, piece after piece, the amount of knowledge he possesses in the end is his destiny. And it is also clear, how he has made it.

Similarly, our action, whether of the body, the speech or the mind, goes in the end, to make our instincts and these instincts reside in our causal bodies. These causal bodies are our destinies. We make them ourselves. They are our earnings.

Any action that we perform perishes as soon as it is complete. But it leaves its impression on our bodily organs as well as on our minds. For example, when, for the first time, we began to write, we took up our pen and put something on the paper or the slate. That action was over. When we repeated a similar action again, our hand as well as our mind began to move in a particular manner. When our practice increased, it produced a habit and we could write with amazing swiftness. How did this habit grow? By constant practice, this is how we make a habit. We could have made another habit quite different from this habit. Habits are rarefied forms of activities. When these habits are very old, they go to form instincts. When we first did an action, we did it at some cost. We had to make efforts. When a thing became a habit, it could be done easily, though with some sort of intention or consciousness. When the habits become permanent, they cause instincts. An instinctive act needs no effort. Up to the stage of habits we make some calculation. When the stage of instincts is reached, the question of calculation disappears. We do it automatically. Why? Because our causal body has been so molded by our actions, that the outer bodies have to obey its behests. It is not difficult to see that our instincts do not belong to grosser bodies. They simply find their expression through them.

Thus we are the makers of our causal bodies, which is our destiny. These causal bodies show at what particular stage of development we are. They show our innermost nature, which is ourselves. It is the end of our whole life. Whatever we thought, whatever we spoke, and whatever we did was all for this end.

Just as every vocation or calling we follow including the smallest details goes to make our income or earning, they being the end or goal of our calling. Similarly, every thought, word, or action goes to build our innermost or causal body, which is our destiny.

When we die, this causal body consists of all our belongings. It is ours. All else is left behind, relatives, money, house, the gross body and even the subtle body. They were simply the means and not the end.

This destiny or causal body is the end of this life as well as the beginning of the next life. It is the pound we got in exchange of our pennies. We take it with us and embark on our fresh journey. This pound of ours begins to bring fresh pennies for us in the new life. This is the fructification of our karma. Our present life is the fruit of our past karma and our future life will be the fruit of our present karma.

Thus, the cycle of karma and life goes on, just as a seed of wheat when sown and nurtured brings other seeds and these seeds in their turn produce their descendants. From seed to fruit and from fruit to seed, the cycle goes on *ad infinitum*, from eternity to eternity.

III

The Death Experience

by James S. Perkins

[*Mr. Perkins was President of the Theosophical Society in America from 1945 to 1960.*]

As a person lives within himself, so does he die; he carries through the gateway of death the entire inner content of his life—its most potent element, that of his motivating aspirations. Another point to be aware of in all deaths, and especially the shockingly violent cases, is that physical pain is impossible from the instant the *silver cord* is broken. This is the thread of specialized life-matter that links higher consciousness with the physical body throughout the incarnation. From the moment this link is snapped, the individual is "dead" to the physical world. As long as the cord remains intact, it is possible for one to return to the physical body, becoming conscious in it again.

Any one of us may encounter sudden death in a wreck or a calamity or when merely walking along the street. This latter kind of experience befell the author in a manner so violent as to involve all the factors of sudden death at a moment when consciousness, by contrast, was fully engaged with preoccupations at the opposite extreme of violence. Because this occurrence has documentary value about the subject under consideration, perhaps the following personal account of its significant features may be usefully introduced at this point.

The accident took place upon a paved highway on a cold, sunny afternoon. The wind was blowing so that my coat collar was turned up causing all sounds to blend with the rush of wind in my ears. I was walking along the shoulder of the road facing traffic, if there had been any. No car was in sight when, crossing the road, I began my return journey. In a quiet, happy state of mind, deeply engaged with perceptions of beauty in the surroundings, I was completely unaware of a car that was now swiftly approaching from the rear. Its driver was asleep at the wheel, and the automobile was edging over to the wrong side of the road and onto the shoulder where I strode along without the slightest premonition of impending disaster. Suddenly, with unabated speed, the car struck my body, smashing my legs with its bumper, head and shoulders with its radiator and hood, then flinging the body some fifteen feet along the road to land head first on the pavement where it slid to a rest. As far as I was concerned, the body had been violently killed while in full and free action, and while I was mentally focused in regions of abstract awareness. Unconsciousness continued for several days, with life in doubt, while the body was in the hospital.

Unbroken Self-Identity

This detailed description enables me to give full weight to the categorical statement that there was no experience whatever of pain, not the slightest ripple of fear or horror, no agonized feeling of any kind. I had been intently preoccupied with perceptions of beauty and the deep sense of joyousness that usually accompanies such contemplation, when suddenly personal consciousness disappeared into boundless universality. The merging was instantaneous, with no awareness of blankness or blackout, only of transition into a shoreless ocean of life and light, an unobstructed wholeness, radiant with love and power unending. The arresting factor was the unbroken sense of self-identity. Without bewilderment or anxiety, with only the clearest assurance that *death was not*, I was alive in a universe of light. There, streams of Divine Force are seen raying downward into the worlds below, and at the physical level every living thing is seen channeling these radiations of light.

Apparently every flower, tree, animal, and human being has evolved its physical body as a perfect anchorage in physical matter for radiating these forces that are constantly influencing and changing the world about us. Although my consciousness during the coma was located in the higher realms indicated, I found that I could descend at times into the physical brain to deliver some communication. But in each instance, consciousness returned at once to the formless world where it was centered. The center was there, not here in the brain and body. Even though the *silver cord* was not broken, consciousness was performing as though it had been reoriented as a result of death.

The sojourn that I am describing lasted for several days, during which it became clear that man cannot live fully and continuously in that awesome region until he has awakened and unfolded his consciousness to cosmic proportions.

The Growth to Godhood

The growth to Godhood is a gradual process, requiring ages of evolutionary effort, of innumerable relationships that call into expression every potential of love and lawful being. How precious, then, becomes each relationship with family and kin, with companions and associates, and with all whom we actively contact, friends and enemies alike. Each challenges some additional aspect of our nature, evokes some new facet of our capacity to love and to understand.

No less important in this unfoldment of the inner divine Self, are the relationships we have with nature, with all living creatures, each radiating some measure of the entire forces that compose the ocean of being in which we exist and share in the one life of God. All relationships throughout time are assisting in the awakening and unfolding of each individual's latent powers, his capacity to dwell forever in omniscient, omnipresent Consciousness.

Reasonably disposed, therefore, is this school of life in which we reincarnate in changing patterns of relationships, sometimes as husband and wife, again as child and parent, or brother and sister, pupil and teacher, disciple and master—and in all these many wonderful ways discovering together the higher dimensions of Divine Love and Cosmic Consciousness.

During the several days spent in this profound retreat, a change took place in the mysterious depths of my consciousness. Movement earthward seemed to begin with an urge toward further sentient experience. The center of consciousness moved "downward," level by level, as in the process of reincarnation, reaching at length and becoming established again in the heavy brain and body. I found, then, that it was possible to journey in thought and being to where I had been, but the center of consciousness was now changed, anchored in the physical form, returning to it from whatever excursions were attempted.

The Illusionary Pageant

Having "reincarnated" so to speak, there followed a curious period of reluctance to resume interest in the illusionary pageant of earth life. (The most insistent impression brought back from "outside" physical existence is that of perceiving the completeness of our state of illusion while blanketed in the physical body.) The perspectives that give meaning to every detail of life had been opened, however, and these provided fresh motivation for effort.

The personal experience just recited seems to confirm several important points that have been noted previously as we have reviewed the subject of death and the conditions immediately following. For one thing, the whole cycle of the human situation was clearly etched: The reincarnating self was known in its own realm by the instantaneous leap of consciousness to its highest abode at the moment of its release; then in due course was experiencing the "thirst," or need for sentient existence that begins the process of reincarnation. Following this, there was a conscious return into the limited personal outlook, sheltered in its carapace of flesh, submerged in the ocean of material illusion.

The illusion is complete mainly because of our instinctive identification of consciousness with the physical body and material world. How natural it is for us to be certain that we see with our eyes and hear with our ears—together with the brain centers with which these organs are connected, physiologists will add. There is no questioning the fact that anyone deprived of eyes and ears can no longer see and hear. If there is a report of a blind man who can "see" in another way, or of a deaf person who "hears" in some extraordinary manner, this is interpreted as some form of sublimation of physical reality, if not of imagining, or hallucination. At all events, it cannot be normal sight and hearing, and therefore cannot be equated with reality as physically sensed.

It is here that the illusion of matter takes hold, for we mistakenly identify all of reality with senate experience. Throughout time man has commonly measured real existence in physical terms. But human consciousness, in the course of evolution, is evolving subtler awareness of reality and contact with it in greater and lesser measures. Even now it is understandable that the sense of sight, hearing, and touch are merged in a *supersense* of "magnetics," of identification through vibratory rapport, or resonances. We employ a number of terms to report such consciousness. The words harmony, empathy, unity, and the inclusive term *love*, used in its universal, unobstructed meaning, all indicate a super-sensing of Reality (here denoting universal being and becoming, the manifestation of absolute Truth).

With the death of the physical body, consciousness, released from identification with sense-reality, does not simply disappear into nothingness, or into some condition associated with flimsy imagining. Consciousness "goes" magnetically to the level of reality in which it is already centered. The magnetics are fixed at all times whether we are "living" or "dead"—fixed by the sum total of consciousness of the self in this mundane and universal region of being. . . .

What has been said here appears to have validity in view of the experiences accompanying the accident described above. For example, there is the strangely significant fact that my consciousness was never anywhere near the scene of the accident, not even momentarily. It continued to be where it was oriented at the moment of the accident: namely, in an abstract formless region of the inner worlds where joyous unity prevails. From this, it follows as an inevitable implication, that we go, after death, where we already are in our inner life. Heaven and hell are states of consciousness that we create, and have the power to recreate. Many thinkers have said as much.

The Final Contemplations

Another point inviting attention is that my state of consciousness not only had no traffic with the physical scene, but bypassed similarly, both the etheric and astral conditions—in fact, every level of form. Here illustrated, it seems, is the importance of one's outlook at the moment of death. Death approaches each one, offering the greatest opportunity of the whole incarnation for one to rise into and sustain a high peak of realization, the effect of which will surely benefit subsequent conditions.

This observation gives significance to Tibetan ideas concerning the opportunity that is available to everyone at the time of death. Their ideas will be found especially interesting to the reader who is giving careful attention to the subject. According to Tibetan custom the administering priest seeks to enjoin in the dying person an achievement of the highest possible level of consciousness in meditation, and the sustaining of it just before the moment of death. The effect of this willed effort is to project the person at once, after death, into the sublime life of the immortal Self.

A final point to be mentioned because of its theosophical connotations, is the lasting result of the experience related above. This can be described as a state of "high-tension relief," that is to say, of relief as to the wondrous life surrounding us and stretching limitlessly ahead of us, to be realized in ever deepening measure. Therefore, there is no need for the anxieties and fears that beset us as to our ultimate fate.

The term "high-tension relief" is meant to indicate a condition of keyed-up awareness, or energized volition, which slides back the imprisoning canopy of physical limitation, and breathes the air of *conscious immortality*. The effects permeate all levels of the lower self with a spreading sense of relief and of reattunement with that enduring quality that in nature is recognized as timeless patience.

IV

Existence
After Death

by Swami Chinmayananda

The question of whether there is existence after death or not has been a fascinating topic for writers and philosophers in every age. But even highly intellectual thinkers find it difficult to deal with this question because it is not one that belongs to the realm of the mind and intellect. Such transcendental questions cannot be explained by words, or established through any of the ordinarily known "proofs of knowledge" such as direct perception, comparison, and inference. The only way to solve these questions is through the words of wisdom given out by persons of realization, such as the saints and sages.

In the *Bhagavad Gītā,* the poet-philosopher Vyasa recorded the Vedic truths as given out by Lord Krishna to Arjuna in the battlefield of life. Lord Krishna takes the mind of Arjuna in His hands, and, in the end, completely cures him from all his neurotic tendencies. As part of these teachings, the perennial issue of life and death is exhaustively dealt with. The topic of reincarnation is introduced in the second chapter where Lord Krishna indicates that death is the total divorce of the subtle body from its physical structure. Therefore, death is the destiny of the body and not a tragedy of our continuing personality.

In Hinduism it has always been emphasized that there is continuity of existence after death. An individual continues in a new embodiment and environment after the death of the physical form. The individuality which undergoes the experiences of birth and death repeatedly, is called the *jīva*. This *jīva* is the eternal light of Consciousness playing upon and *seemingly* conditioned by the subtle body comprised of the mind and intellect. This subtle body, which is nothing but a bundle of thoughts, moves out of the physical body when its purpose has been exhausted. Even while living in this body, thoughts determine both our physical and subtle movements. And after death we still pursue the fulfillment of those thoughts which we had while acting through the body.

When we call the bank for the balance of our account, we do not expect to get the total sum of money that we had deposited in the past, but only the current balance. Similarly, the result of motives and intentions encouraged, positive and negative thoughts entertained, and actions performed, determine the type and texture of our thoughts when we leave the physical body.

Types of Thought

In the fourteenth chapter of the *Gītā,* Lord Krishna defines three types of thought-textures, or *guṇas*, through which the human mind functions: *Sattva*—purity: thoughts that are pure and noble; *Rajas*—passion: thoughts that are passionate and agitated; and *Tamas*—inertia: thoughts that are dull and inactive.

The quality of thoughts is influenced by the type of *guṇa* behind them. Our predominant *guṇa* is cultivated by the type of activities and thoughts that we engage in throughout our lives. Therefore, it is logical to assume that the predominant *guṇa* also determines the direction and range of the subtle body after its release from the physical body. This is explained in the following verse from the *Gītā*:

> *If the embodied one meets death when* sattva *is predominant, then he attains the spotless world of the knowers of the Highest.* (XIV:14)

25

Lord Krishna now gives us an idea of the direction of the mind and intellect after death. This can already be determined by closely watching a person's behavior during his or her life. A doctor cannot suddenly think of and solve a subtle architectural problem. Nor can an engineer discover a cure for a disease overnight. The doctor has trained his mind along the lines of medicine and disease, and the engineer has trained himself to solve the problems of building design. Both the doctor and the engineer will always be thinking in conformity with their education.

Thus, there is a continuity of thought-life in this embodiment. This year's thoughts have a continuity with last year's thoughts, and today's thoughts are continued tomorrow. Every moment is an extension of the previous moment's thoughts. Thus, if there is continuous development in the thought-life during one's embodiment, then there is no reason why this continuity should suddenly end at the time of death.

If *sattva* predominates, then one attains to the highest heavenly realm. This is a field of abundant joy, unaffected by excessive *rajas* or *tamas*. The following verse describes what happens when one departs while in *rajas* or *tamas:*

> *Meeting death in* rajas *he is born among those attached to action; and dying in* tamas, *he is born in the womb of the senseless.* (XIV:15)

If, at the time one leaves the body, the mind is under the influence of *rajas*, it takes an embodiment among those who are extremely attached to action. If, on the other hand, one dies when one's mind is overpowered by extreme *tamas*, one goes to the lower realms of beings, such as the animal and vegetable kingdoms. The mind seeks the most appropriate field where it can exhaust its existing tendencies.

Once we have evolved to the status of human beings, it is perhaps consoling to believe that we shall never fall to a lower state. But this is not what we see when we observe the world around us. We find that people, even while in the best of environments, do not make good use of their circumstances. And as a result they do not evolve culturally.

We are all born as rational beings, but how many of us behave with proper discrimination? Sometimes we even envy the lives of certain animals. When such ideas are entertained in one's mind, the life of an animal is not devolution, but only an acquisition of something that one is thirsting for. For *tamasic* persons to be born in the animal kingdom is a wonderful opportunity for exhausting their cravings.

The Path of Liberation

All experiences of the finite world, with the accompanying joys and sorrows, constitute the *saṁsāra* of the ego. And ego is nothing other than the three *guṇas* present in each of us.

True release or liberation (*mokṣa*) takes place not only when the *guṇas* are transcended, but also when we have become fully established in the spiritual experience. This is just like a patient with a virus who suffers from three symptoms: a high temperature, headache, and body pain. It is only when the patient has regained his former health and energy that we can say that he has completely recovered, and not when the three symptoms have ended.

Each of us seeks to overcome the limitations of the *guṇas* in order to experience the greater possibilities inherent in us. By doing so we overcome our self-imposed prison of confusion, pain, agitations, and sorrows. To stand apart from the mind by ending all our identification with it, is to obtain complete freedom from our thought-entanglements. Describing the path of liberation, the Lord says:

> *When the seer beholds no agent other than the* guṇas *and knows That which is higher than the* guṇas, *he attains to My Being.* (XIV:19)

The art of dissociating ourselves from our own thought processes is the art of meditation. An accomplished meditator will behold, experience subjectively, the state of pure Knowledge, uncontaminated by the dance of thoughts. It is called seeing, but not in the sense that one sees an object. For God cannot be seen. He is not an object of our perception, feeling, or thought. He is the subject because of whom we perceive, feel, and think.

Here the word "behold" is used only to indicate that the subjective experience shall be as complete and convincing as when we have actually seen an object. After having had this experience, there is no more any speculation about it!

The experiencer of the Self not only realizes himself to be the Infinite, but also understands that his ego, which previously claimed to be the agent in all his activities, was none other than these *guṇas*. *Guṇas* govern and direct our entire thought life at all times.

The mind, being a by-product of inert matter, cannot function of its own accord. Consciousness which functions in and through the mind, making it brilliant and dynamic, must be a principle that is other than the mind. If a bucket of water looks like molten silver, it must have borrowed the brilliance from the sun or the moon, as water by itself has no brilliance. If the reflection dances or breaks up, it must be because of the nature of the water in the bucket and not because the sun is dancing in the sky. Consciousness reflecting in the mind is the agent, the individualized ego (*jīva*) in us, who suffers the self-shattering torments of *saṁsāra* (cycle of births and deaths).

He who understands that he is not the reflection in his own mind, but That which is reflected therein, is the one who has escaped the shackles of all limitations forever. He has discovered himself to be That which was giving the capacity to the mind to delude itself. That person of wisdom merges with the Self.

A waker when he goes to sleep comes to lose and gain, weep

and smile in his dream. All his joys and sorrows belong to him as the dreamer. When awake, the dream and its sorrows end, and the dreamer himself becomes the waker. When you, the dreamer, behold no agent other than the dreaming mind you shall attain to my being—the waking consciousness.

Similarly here, Krishna, the manifested God-Consciousness is explaining to us that our egocentric life and activities, along with its joys and sorrows, belong to the waker-dreamer-sleeper personality. On transcending them all, we shall awake to the Truth, and become one with It. A dreamer, on waking, cannot remain a dreamer but must himself become the waker. Similarly, the Self entangled in matter is man, and man disentangled from matter identification not only rediscovers, but also attains the Self. "He attains to My being."

The Lord now further elaborates on the effect of gaining this great goal:

> *The embodied one, having crossed beyond these three* guṇas, *out of which the body is evolved, is freed from birth, death, decay, and pain, and attains to Immortality.* (XIV:19)

The three *guṇas* are the expressions of ignorance or nescience, which constitute the causal body. We experience the pure causal body in our deep sleep. The *guṇas* emerge from the causal body to express themselves first as the subtle body, as thoughts and feelings, and again, as the gross body as good, bad, or indifferent actions.

If I am to express an artistic ability in me, I need a canvas and brush. If I am a musician, I need musical instruments to express my art. Artists require appropriate means to express themselves. A violin in the hands of a painter, or a brush and canvas in the hands of a musician are both useless because they are not the right means of expression.

If my thoughts are dull and animalistic, it would be painful for me to have a human body. Thus, each body—plant, animal, or human—is the exact instrument given for the full expression of its subtle body. And the nature of the subtle body is determined by the texture of the causal body, consisting of the *guṇas*. Therefore, those who have gone beyond the *guṇas* are no more suffering from the tragedies of the subtle and causal bodies.

Matter changes forever and these changes have been systematized into the five definite stages of birth, growth, decay, disease, and death. They are common to all bodies everywhere, and each one is full of pain. But these sorrows are only the sorrows of matter and not of the Consciousness that illumines them. The sun may illumine floods, famine, war, pestilence, funerals, marriages and a million varieties of happenings, and yet, none of these can affect the sun. Similarly, the Consciousness in us illumines the various changes that we experience throughout life, but they do not pertain to the Self.

In deep sleep, a person who is suffering forgets his pain, and one who is hungry does not feel his hunger. But neither is illness cured, nor hunger satisfied by one's going to sleep. Sleep is a temporary truce with the existing world of sorrows within, but upon waking the sorrows return. The state of Self-realization, however, is not a temporary cessation from the sorrows of life, but a permanent experience of the joy of the changeless, infinite Self. Therefore, it is said here that one "attains to immortality," even while living in this embodiment.

PART TWO

Concepts of
Heaven and Hell

*There is a different
heaven and hell
for each person,
in accordance with the grade
of his evolution.*

Hazrat Inayat Khan

There are no coincidences. God is not a punitive, nasty God. After you make the transition, then you come to what has been described as hell and heaven. What we hear from our friends who have passed over, people who came back to share with us, is that every human being, after this transition, is going to have to face something that looks very much like a television screen.

You will be given an opportunity—not to be judged by a judgmental God—but to judge yourself, by having to review every single action, every word, and every thought of your life. You make your own hell or your own heaven by the way you have lived.

Elizabeth Kubler Ross
Life After Death

V

Judgment

by Leslie D. Weatherhead

[*The author wrote "The Christian Agnostic," from which this article was reprinted, after he retired from active ministry in the Methodist Church.*]

No words used in the Gospels can legitimately be twisted to mean unending punishment, and indeed, such an expression is self-contradictory. The main motive of punishment surely is to reform the sufferer: in school, to make a better scholar, and in the state, to make a better citizen. If punishment goes on forever, when does the sufferer benefit by the punishment or use the lessons he has learned so painfully? If hell were endless it would be valueless.

Yet for myself I do not dismiss the imagery of fire. I cannot, for our Lord introduced it, however His followers may have distorted it. And there is a compliment implied in the very use of the word "fire." Wood, hay, and stubble are *destroyed* by fire. (Corinthians 3:12-15) Gold is refined by it. Since destruction cannot be God's plan, his use of a discipline comparable with fire points to man's character being of the nature of gold that benefits by it. Nor does one forget that the refiner of gold carries the purifying process to the point at which he can *see his own face* in the molten metal. ("I shall be satisfied when I awake in Thy likeness." Psalm 17:15)

And while there is much in the Roman Catholic idea of purgatory that I cannot accept, such as indulgences and ability to

shorten it by costly gifts. I know my own heart well enough to
know that there is much in my nature that must be "burned
away" before I can become all that I want to be and am capable
of being. And surely the latter is God's plan and my goal, to be
made all that He can make me, and to become at last with Him
in an unbroken unity of communion and purpose.

Dr. Austin Farrer says it well, "Purgatory was rejected by
our reformers as undermining the sufficiency of Christ's atonement; for it was taken to be the serving of a sentence by which
the guilt of Christians was in some way worked off. Such an
objection has no force against the teaching that we have a pain to
pass through, in being reconciled to truth and love. And we may
as well call this pain purgatorial, having no other name to call it.
It seems strange indeed that so practical and pressing a truth as
that of purgatory should be dismissed, while so remote and
impractical a doctrine as the absolute everlastingness of hell
should be insisted on. Nor is it that ultimate fire is scriptural,
while remedial fire is not. Remedial fire was taught plainly
enough by St. Paul to his Corinthians."[1]

Of course, the human soul will always have the power to
reject God, for choice is essential to its nature, but I cannot
believe that anyone will finally do this. To enter the next phase
after death feeling very "out of it" and not even wanting to be "in
it," in fellowship and love with others; to take no steps to "see
the Kingdom of Heaven"—to use a phrase Jesus seems often to
have used—to have no aspiration toward the heights of being,
even when their glories are more fully revealed, seems
impossible to me. If it were successful, there could be no perfect
heaven for anyone, for we cannot complacently enjoy God if
one of His sons or daughters is finally lost, and He Himself
defeated in His aims. For as Paul wrote to Timothy, "He willeth
that all men should be saved and come to the knowledge of
the Truth." (1 Timothy 2:4) It may take aeons, as we think of
time, or even many reincarnations, but we have the highest
authority for believing that the Great Shepherd Himself will not

be content if one of His sheep is missing from the final fold. . . .

Alone With Our Conscience

I never think of the afterlife as all suffering or all pleasure,
but very much like this life with light and shadow intermingled.
But periods of self-discovery there must be and they may well
be "hell" as we remember, and, with a new power of spiritual
insight, reassess the sins we so glibly committed. Forgiveness
will restore the relationship between ourselves and God. But as
we remember our sins and assess the costliness of restoration,
surely an experience of a burning sorrow will sting our hearts
with purging pain. We read of a "book being opened" and ourselves judged (Revelation 20:12), but the book will be the book
of our own memory, and the judge our own awakened conscience.

> I sat alone with my conscience,
> In a place where time had ceased;
> We discoursed of my former living
> In a land where the years increased.
> And I felt I should have to answer
> The questions it put to me,
> And to face those questions and answers
> In that dim eternity.
>
> And the ghosts of forgotten actions
> Came floating before my sight,
> And the sins that I thought were dead sins
> Were alive with a terrible might.
> And I know of the future judgment,
> How dreadful so'er it be,
> That to sit alone with my conscience
> Would be judgment enough for me.[2]

But for every sin, forgiveness is offered; in every heart re-
pentance, recovery, and progress are possible as truly after death
as before it. What is there in the trivial incident of dying to prevent this? When we catch from Christ even a glimpse of what we

can be made, by grace through discipline, and by grace through sunshine, we shall understand a phrase that used to puzzle me from the old saints and scholars: "The soul will run to its punishment."[3] Yes, burning may well be the way to bliss. If so, God help us to run to the fire!

An old legend puts the matter vividly: A man dreamed one night that he was allowed to pass into the next world. When he arrived an angel invited him to visit heaven and hell, and together they went through all the courts of heaven. The things they saw were very wonderful and very beautiful. But the heart of the visitor was ill at ease for he thought to himself, "This is all very fine, but how can they enjoy it while their brethren suffer in yonder torment?" And the angel read his very thoughts and said, "Would you like to see the place they call hell?" And, trembling a little, the visitor said that he would. So it came to pass that they drew near the gates of hell. The flames were terrible, and so great a heat was thrown out that the visitor thought, "We shall not get near enough to see anything." And again the angel read his thoughts and said, "But can you not hear anything?" And to his surprise the visitor heard strange and beautiful music coming from the heart of the fire. And he said to his angelic guide, "Sir, tell me, what wondrous songs are these that the souls in hell itself are singing?" And the angel whispered softly in his ear, "They are the songs of the redeemed."

FOOTNOTES:

[1] Austin Farrer, *Saving Belief*, p. 154.
[2] Bishop Charles W. Stubbs, formerly Bishop of Truro.
[3] Plato's phrase, "The soul will run eagerly to its judge," and that of Hegel, "The sinful soul has a right to its punishment." See also my *Psychology, Religion and Healing*, pp. 325-27.

39

VI

Heaven and Hell

by Meher Baba

After death there is no consciousness of the gross world for the ordinary soul, since such consciousness is directly dependent on the physical body. Though the consciousness of the gross world is thus lost, the impressions of the experiences of the gross world are retained in the mental body; and they continue to express themselves through the semi-subtle world. During the interval between death and next incarnation, the consciousness of the soul is turned toward these impressions resulting in a vivification of impressions and the revival of corresponding experiences. However, this soul does not become aware of the subtle environment; it is wrapped up in complete subjectivity and absorbed in living through the revived impressions.

In life after death the experiences of pain and pleasure become much more intense than they were in earthly life. These subjective states of intensified suffering and joy are called hell and heaven. Hell and heaven are states of mind; they should not be looked upon as being places. And though subjectively they mean a great deal to the individualized soul, they are both illusions within the greater illusion.

In the hell state as well as in the heaven state, desires become much more intense since they no longer require expression through the gross medium. Like desires, the experiences incurred in their fulfillment or nonfulfillment also become greatly intensified. In the earthly career, desires, as well as the pleasures and the sufferings they bring, are experienced through the medium of the gross body. The soul is, of course, actually using its higher bodies at the same time, but in the earthly career its consciousness is bound up with the gross body. Therefore the processes of consciousness have to pass through an additional veil that lessens their force, liveliness, and intensity—just as rays of light are dimmed when they are required to pass through a thick glass. During habitation in the body, desires and experiences suffer a deterioration in intensity; but when that habitation is given up, they undergo a relative increase of intensity.

In the heaven state the fulfillment of desires is not, as in the gross sphere, dependent upon having the object of desire. Fulfillment of desire comes merely through thinking of the object desired. For example, if a person wishes to hear exquisite music, he experiences this pleasure merely by thinking about it. The imaginative idea of exquisite music becomes, in this state, a substitute for the physical sound vibrations in the gross sphere. The pleasure he derives from the thought of exquisite music is much greater than the pleasure he derived in his earthly career from the actual hearing of physical sounds. In the heaven state there are no obstacles between desires and their fulfillment; the pleasure of self-fulfillment through thought or feeling is always at hand.

In fact, even in the earthly sphere of existence some individuals develop this capacity of making their pleasure independent of possession of a gross object. Beethoven, for example, was completely deaf and yet through the exercise of imagination alone, he was able to enjoy intensely his own compositions of music. In a sense, even on earth he might figuratively be said to have been in the heaven state. In the same way, a person who meditates on the beloved with love derives happiness merely through the thought of the beloved, without requiring a physical presence. After death, in the heaven state, the enjoyment of such imaginative fulfillment is infinitely greater since consciousness is then unburdened of the outermost veil of the gross body.

Coarse Desires Cause Suffering

Some desires have a direct relation to the possession and assimilation of gross objects through the gross body. The coarser desires such as lust, gluttony, or the craving for alcohol or drugs are of this type. These desires are specifically earthly because they are possessive and they involve an element of clinging to a physical object. In these desires there is not only a preponderance of sensations derived from contact with the object but also of those sensations that constitute the response of the body itself. These coarser desires contribute to the hell state.

In contrast with the finer desires, the coarser desires place an infinitely heavier premium on mere sensations, quite independently of any intellectual meaning or moral value. In the finer desires, such as the desire for music, there is, of course, an element of wanting sense contact with the physical sounds. But these sounds become important not so much in their own right as in their capacity to express beauty. In the same way, a desire to hear discourses has a hold upon the mind, not so much because of the sensations of sound, but because of the intellectual meaning and emotional appeal they convey.

Thus in the finer desires, the actual sensations play a subordinate role to the derivative aspects based upon the sensations. In the coarser desires the chief element is provided by the actual sensations connected with the physical object and the sensations aroused by them through bodily response to their possession. The organic sensations of the physical body play the greatest part in experiences connected with the coarser desires. Through them the individualized soul feels its own existence as the gross body much more effectively and vividly than through experiences connected with finer desires.

Almost the entire significance of experiences brought about by the fulfillment or nonfulfillment of coarser desires is constituted by the *bodily* sensations themselves. Therefore, they can rarely yield the full experience of fulfillment achieved through finer desires merely by the exercise of thought and imagination. It is characteristic of the coarser desires to insist on the possession and assimilation of the gross objects themselves. Any imaginative idea of the gross objects merely serves the purpose of accentuating the urge to reach out to them. Since the gross objects of the coarser desires are not available in the semi-subtle world, these desires are mostly productive of an intensified experience of the suffering of nonfulfillment. Just as in the gross world the presence of coarser desires leads to the preponderance of suffering over pleasure, in the life after death the revived experiences connected with these coarser desires also lead to a preponderance of suffering over pleasure—thus bringing into existence the hell state. Similarly, in the life after death the revived experiences connected with the finer desires lead to a preponderance of pleasure over suffering, thus bringing into existence the heaven state.

States of Bondage

Hell and heaven are both states of bondage, however, and subject to the limitations of the opposites of pleasure and pain. Both are states whose duration is determined by the nature, amount, and intensity of the accumulated impressions. Time in the semi-subtle world is not the same as time in the gross world due to the increased subjectivity of the states of consciousness. Though time in the semi-subtle world is thus incommensurable with time in the gross world, it is strictly determined by the impressions accumulated in the gross world. However, the important fact is that the hell state and the heaven state are far from being lasting, and after they have served their purpose in the life of the individualized soul, they both come to an end.

The coarser sensual desires, like lust and their emotional products like hate and anger, all contribute to the life of delusion and suffering prevalent in the hell state. The finer desires—like idealistic aspirations, aesthetic and scientific interests, goodwill toward neighbors and others, and their emotional products like personal love or fellow-feeling—contribute to the life of enlightenment and pleasure prevalent in the heaven state. These states for most souls consist in reliving the experiences of the earthly life by vivification of the impressions left by them. Their duration and nature are dependent upon the duration and nature of the experiences undergone by the soul while in the physical body.

Just as a phonograph record is set aside after the needle has traveled through each groove, the hell state and the heaven state terminate after consciousness has traversed the imprints left by earthly life. Just as the song produced by the record is strictly determined by the original song recorded on it, the quality of intensified and magnified experiences the soul passes through after death is strictly determined by the kind of life that was led on earth in the physical body. From this point of view, heaven and hell are shadows cast by one's earthly life.

Assimilation of Experiences

Heaven and hell would, however, serve no specially useful purpose in the life of the individual soul if they were to consist merely of mental revival of the earthly past. That would mean bare repetition of what has already occurred. Consciousness in these after-death states is in a position to make a leisurely and effective survey of the animated record of earthly life. Through intensification of experiences, it can observe their nature with better facility and results. On earth, the consciousness of most persons is predominantly objective and forward-looking and under the pressure of unspent *saṁskāras* (desire-impressions). It is most concerned with the possible fulfillment of *saṁskāras* through the present or the future. In life after death the consciousness of most persons is predominantly subjective and retrospective. With the absence of forward-goading *saṁskāras*, it is, as in reminiscences, mostly preoccupied with reviewing and assessing the significance of the past.

The fret and fury of immediate responses to the changing situations of earthly life is replaced in life after death by a more leisurely mood, freed from the urgency of immediately needed actions. All the experiences of the earthly career are now available for reflection in a form more vivid than is possible through memory in earthly life. The shots of earthly life have all been taken on the cinematic film of the mind, and it is now time to study the original earthly life through the magnified projections of the filmed record on the screen of subjectivized consciousness.

Thus the hell state and the heaven state become instrumental in the assimilation of experiences acquired in the earthly phase; and the individualized soul can start its next incarnation in a physical body with all the advantages of digested experience. The lessons learned by the soul through such stocktaking and reflection are confirmed in the mental body by the power of their magnified suffering or happiness. They become, for the next incarnation, an integral part of the intuitive makeup of active consciousness, without in any way involving detailed revival of the individual events of the previous incarnation. The truths absorbed by the mind in the life after death become in the next incarnation a part of inborn wisdom. Developed intuition is consolidated and compressed understanding, distilled through a multitude of diverse experiences gathered in previous lives.

Different souls start with different degrees of intuitive wisdom as their initial capital for the experiments and adventures of their earthly careers. This intuition may seem to have been the product of past experiences, thus adding to the equipment of the psyche; but it is more truly an unfoldment of what was already latent in the individualized soul. From this deeper point of view, the experiences of earthly life—as well as the reflective and consolidating processes they are subjected to in life after death—are merely instrumental in gradually releasing to the surface the intuitive wisdom already latent in the soul from the very beginning of creation. As is true of the earthly career and its experiences, the states of hell and heaven in the life after death are also integral parts of, and incidents in that journey of the individualized soul, which is ultimately meant to reach the Source of all things.

VII

A Visit to Heaven and Hell

by Swami Chinmayananda

Heaven and hell are both created here by our actions. There is no hell except our selfishness. There is no heaven except our own selfless love.

A group of people once wanted to know what makes up hell and heaven. Hell, they heard, is where everybody suffers, and heaven is where all enjoy. So the committee went on a fact-finding mission. First they went to hell and what they saw there took them completely by surprise. Hell looked like a very rich place where every enjoyable object was available in plenty. Why should any one suffer here, they wondered?

As it was lunchtime in hell, all the citizens were in the dining room and so the committee went to investigate whether there was a food problem. The committee member's eyes just about popped out of their heads when they saw the dining room table, as it was full of food and various delicacies. Yet the most puzzling aspect of all was the fact that all the citizens who were gathered at the table looked famished, hungry, and angry. They were quarreling and blaming each other in abusive language.

The members of the investigation committee closely scrutinized the people who were quarreling and fighting. They found that people in hell had no elbow joints in their arms so they could not bend their hands to feed themselves. Therefore, all of them starved and had no joy. The committee felt that it was a cruel joke to play upon people. Why give them plenty of food if it was not meant to feed them?

The Denizens of Heaven

Then they went to see how things were in heaven. They came just in time for dinner. As they approached the dining room they could hear loud cries of satisfaction and joy emanating from the room. The committee members hastened to the dining room to witness an exuberance of joy. To their great surprise heaven looked exactly like hell, very rich, with all the enjoyable things of life. The dining table was full of delicacies just like in hell. But the people looked happy, content, and well-fed.

As they were eating, the committee members scrutinized people's arms carefully and noticed that their arms were also without elbow joints. Just like the citizens in hell, they could not bend their forearms to feed themselves, yet they were happy. They understood that the food in front of them was meant for serving others. So they all collected enough food from the table and fed each other. When each fed the other, all of them had plenty to eat and no one went hungry. All were happy and it became heaven.

The people in hell, however, did not know that their hands were given for serving others. When they tried to serve themselves only, they could not do it and this is why it became hell.

VIII

The Flight of
the Subtle Body

by Swami Chinmayananda

The cardinal philosophical idea in Vedanta is that an individualized ego continues to identify with a given physical body only as long as it needs that particular instrument for gathering its desired quota of experiences. Once it is over, it "kicks the bucket" as it were, and walks off forgetting all its responsibilities, relationships, and vanities of that particular existence. With reference to the body, this condition is called death. But the ego-center, although not manifest and functioning through the body, continues to exist in its subtle form.

This ego-center set in the subtle body is conveyed to its next field of activity (*loka*) by the energy called *udāna*. *Udāna*, which is one of the five *upa prāṇas*, is that energy that supplies the motive power for the ego-center with its subtle body to move out from one physical structure to another at the time of death.

When the subtle body thus divorces from the physical body, it is logical to believe that its thoughts would revolve around the most predominant desire or aspiration in it—either gathered in its past embodiment, or acquired in its present life. This last powerful will, determined by the last thought, decides its destiny in the future.

We are now going to discuss the routes in which evolutionary pilgrimages can be undertaken by the subtle bodies of those individuals who performed self-evolving actions and therefore, were essentially good.

The following verse from the *Praśnopaniṣad* indicates what would be the direction of this flight:

> *. . . And there are two paths: the Southern and the Northern. Those who follow the Path of Karma alone, by the performance of sacrificial and pious acts, obtain only "the world of the Moon" and certainly they are born again . . . . This matter is verily "the path of the ancestors."* (Section I:9)

The "Path of the Ancestors," also known as heaven, is considered to be the path of return, and presided over by the Moon, which represents the world of matter. Those who leave the world after spending their lifetime in doing good and performing rituals, unaccompanied by meditation and worship, are those who go to the world of ancestors.

Vedanta, being thoroughly scientific, has systematically divided every conceivable noble action capable of contributing to the evolution of humankind into two groups: *iṣṭam* and *pūrtam*. *Iṣṭam* comprises those noble acts sanctioned by the scriptural texts called *śrutis*. *Pūrtam* are the noble acts of kindness and charity sanctioned by other subsidiary texts of dharma called *smṛtis*.

Iṣṭam includes all Vedic rituals, self-control, truthfulness, the study of Vedas, disseminating the Vedic knowledge to deserving aspirants, serving unexpected guests, and tending continuously to the sacred fire in the house. *Pūrtam* includes constructing village tanks, public wells, bathing ghats, maintenance or construction of temples, feeding the poor, opening new roads, parks, feeding places, watersheds, and so on. If you analyze these classifications and understand them from the level of the mental condition of the devotees, you will certainly understand how and why they follow two different paths in their evolutionary progress.

Two Classifications of People

Those who are performing *iṣṭam* are individuals of high culture with well-developed intellectual discrimination, who also have a great amount of self-control over sensuous desires. They are mainly people with a contemplative nature, whose only demand in life is to gain greater mental and intellectual perfection. They direct all their efforts toward reaching the final goal of life. Naturally, when they depart from this life, having all the time meditated upon the universal energy aspect of life, their minds identify with the Path of the Sun. And reaching the source of *prāṇa*, cross it, to go beyond.

Those who are performing *pūrtam* actions are also highly cultured members of society. But they are, to a large extent, still entertaining desires for wealth or progeny, or glory and position in life. They are trying to fulfill the small desires of many people through *pūrtam*. By that they expect to be blessed by these satisfied members of the society, and ultimately would obtain fulfillment of their own desires.

Thus, though they lived a noble life of charity, purity, benevolence, and so on, there was always an undercurrent of desire deep within their apparently noble hearts. Their demands were mainly on the material plane. Naturally, when they depart from here they go to the world of matter, the Moon. Thus, following the Southern route they reach the Moon, and crossing it, go to that plane of consciousness called technically as the *pitṛloka*, the world of the manes. There they enjoy supersensuous objects with supersensitive apparatus.

One who has thus gained the heavens as a result of his meritorious acts, after exhausting his merit balance, will have to return to the lower planes of consciousness. And there, pain and struggle, loss and gain, and birth and death will again be his experience. Therefore, the rishi says in the *Muṇḍaka Upaniṣad*:

Engrossed in the ways of the ignorant, these people childishly think that they have gained the end of life. But, being subject to passions and attachments, they never attain Knowledge, and therefore, they fall down wretched, when the fruits of their good deeds are exhausted. (Chapter I, Section II:9.)

In the earlier part of the Vedas, in the *karma kāṇḍa*, there is a sincere advocacy of the performance of karmas. Later, in the Upanishadic portion we find, in stanzas such as these, a vehement condemnation of them. This would look as though it is a palpable contradiction, but it is not.

When children are in an elementary class, you have to insist upon their learning the multiplication tables by heart. But when they come to the standard of pure mathematics, it would be absurd to insist that they practise the multiplication tables every day.

Similarly, rituals have an elementary purpose, without which nothing higher is possible. Yet to continue to devote one's entire life in mere ritualism, would be a terrible waste. Therefore, *śruti* (scripture) is crying down such wasteful policies in spiritual seekers.

It is desire that generates the flow of thoughts in the mind. And it is the quality, texture, quantity, and direction in which thoughts flow, that determine actions. Thus, karma cannot be where desires have ended. Thoughts cannot end where desires have not ceased. Where thoughts are bubbling, the mind must be gross with its dense power.

Therefore, annihilation of the mind is possible only when desires are annihilated. This amounts to saying that these wise, energetic, devoted, and sincere people, in whom ritualism has fulfilled itself, pursue this wrong path of wasteful activity only because of the germs of desires that still breed in their hearts. Thus, the rishi continues:

These ignorant men, who regard sacrificial and charitable acts as most important, do not know any other way to bliss. Having enjoyed in the heights of heaven, the abode of pleasures, they again enter this world or even inferior worlds. (Muṇḍaka Upaniṣad, Chapter I, Section II:10.)

Never was the world without this controversy between the two principles of life, namely, laborious extrovert action (karma) and peaceful introvert seeking (*jñāna*). Karma and *jñāna* have ever been at a tug-of-war, unbroken at all times. This endless controversy itself, we may say, was the main motive-force which gave Hinduism such a perfect and exact science of spirituality. In the history of the world we find periods of karma yielding place to periods of *jñāna*. Which in their turn, give place to karma again after a period of retirement and renunciation.

Meritorious acts are divided into two groups by our ancient rishis, as we have already seen. In the above verse, however, scripture refuses to define the heavens, which are obtained by doing these two types of noble actions, as positive places of happiness. She only says that it is a plane of existence where the soul-killing sorrows of life are not present. She wants us to understand that, though in heaven there are none of the pains of mortal life, it is only relative happiness. The denizens in heaven are only creatures in pain, when their state is compared with the absolute state of perfection, which is the theme of the Upanishads.

In the above verse we also have a positive declaration against the optimistic view held by some of our pundits as well as the most sympathetic of gurus. According to them, once the ego receives the form of a human being, one can never go down to any lower plane of existence, whatever his actions are in life. This idea is being blasted in this mantra. It is also interesting to observe that a person can go down on the ladder of evolution to the existence of even a worm if he engages in deliberate criminal activities.

The Supreme World of the Creator

On the other hand, scripture promises perfect evolutionary success to those rare few who have gained the required spirit of renunciation. As the following verse states:

But those who perform tapas *and* śraddhā *in the forest, having control over their senses, who are learned and living the life of mendicants, go through the orb of the sun, their good and bad deeds being consumed, where the immortal and undecaying* Puruṣa *is.* (Muṇḍaka Upaniṣad, Chapter I, Section II:2.)

It is a Vedantic theory that those who merely perform karmas, on departing from here, take to the Southern path to live in *pitṛloka*. And after enjoying it for a period of time they come back. Those who not only perform the *yajñas* and *yāgas*, but also meditate upon the great Truth of Vedantic philosophy (that is, those who perform karma and *upāsana*), leave the body and take the Northern route. Through the corridors of the Sun they go beyond and enter *Brahmaloka*, the supreme world of the Creator.

It is the belief that they along with the Creator, at the end of the yuga, during the *pralaya* (dissolution), become merged with the supreme absolute Awareness. This method of liberation is technically called *krama mukti* (gradual liberation). But in the case of Buddha, Shankara, Ramakrishna Paramahamsa, Ramana Maharshi, Aurobindo and other masters, there is no coming or going; they reach what is called pure liberation (*kaivalya mukti*) or immediate liberation (*sadyo mukti*).

The theory of gradual liberation accepted by Vedanta, says that ritualism (karma) accompanied by meditation (*upāsana*) takes the ego to the realm of the Creator (*Brahmaloka*). This is where, at the end of the *kalpa* (the cycle of creation and dissolution) it merges with the Supreme. Even in *Brahmaloka* it is necessary that the ego must, through self effort, live strictly all the spiritual directions of the Creator. And through constant contemplation upon the Self, come to deserve the total liberation, by ending all its connections with ignorance. Those who have not reached the realm of the Creator, may not come to enjoy the supreme merger. They will, at the end of the cycle, have to come back and take their manifestation in embodiments, ordered by the remaining *vāsanās*. Keeping this principle in mind, Lord

Krishna says in the *Gītā* that rebirth is for everyone, even for those who have attained the higher planes up to *Brahmaloka.* Having reached *Brahmaloka*, however, there is no return and the *jīvā* rises to merge with the Self.

> *Worlds up to the world of Brahmaji, are subject to rebirth. O Arjuna, but he who reaches Me, O Kaunteya, has no birth again.* (Gītā, Chapter VIII:16)

To those who have awakened to the rediscovery of their eternal nature, and realized themselves to be the one, all-pervading Self, there is no return to the plane of limited existence. To the waker there is no more readmission into the dream-realm. To awaken is to drop forever the joys and sorrows of the dream. After attaining the wakerhood (Me) there is no return into the dreamland *(saṁsāra).*

PART THREE

The Goal of Life

*So I have abandoned
all I ever sought to be.
And in dying my soul has been released.*

St. John of the Cross

The Lord is not asking us to build His kingdom in heaven; it is already well established there and has been since the creation of the world. But he is asking us to establish it on earth, amongst our fellow human beings, by learning to manifest divine virtues. All great masters and initiates know that they have come to earth to work for the establishment of the kingdom of God. A teaching that urges men and women to abandon the earth on the pretext that it is a vale of tears, and that their true homeland is elsewhere, is not in conformity with God's plans. As far as we can tell from all that the great initiates have taught, God's will is that His kingdom should be established on earth.

The task of human beings is to fashion and refine matter and make it so sensitive and subtle that it becomes capable of vibrating in harmony with the world of the spirit. . . . Only when human beings break the bonds that tie them to their lower nature and emerge into the immensity of their higher nature, will they vibrate in unison with the universe. And when that day comes they will receive all the beneficial influences of the cosmos, for thanks to this unison, the channels through which heavenly forces can circulate and flow will be restored.

Omraam Mikhaël Aïvanhov
Daily Meditations

IX

The Internal Death

by Swami Tyagananda

It is in the inner world that we must choose our death, *before* death chooses us in the external world. The only way to neutralize the terror of death is to "die" before we die. This was also the teaching of the Prophet Muhammad. He said, "Be in the world like a traveler, or like a passer-on, and reckon yourself as of the dead."

Abraham von Frankenberg (d.1652) warned: "Who dies not before dying, perishes when he dies." His disciple Daniel von Czepko (b.1605), a mystic poet, expressed the same idea in a different way: "She cannot die, for she died before her death, in order to be living when she died."

Yekiwo, the sixteenth century Japanese Zen Master, taught: "If you are really desirous of mastering Zen, it is necessary for you to once give up your life and to plunge right into the pit of death."

In our own times, Sri Ramakrishna made the idea clear through his life. His disciples found him one day in a high state of *samādhi*, addressing the Divine Mother about his own approaching illness: "O Mother, what will You accomplish by killing one who is already dead?"

A story from the *Bhāgavatam* that Sri Ramakrishna narrated often, will make it easy for us to understand what it is that prevents us from dying before our death.

In a certain place the fishermen were catching fish. A kite [also known as a hawk] swooped down and snatched a fish.

At the sight of the fish, about a thousand crows chased the kite and made a great noise with their cawing. Whichever way the kite flew with the fish, the crows followed it. The kite flew to the south and the crows followed it there. The kite flew to the north and still the crows followed it. The kite went east and west but with the same result. As the kite began to fly about in confusion, lo, the fish dropped from its mouth. The crows at once left the kite alone and flew after the fish. Thus relieved of its worries, the kite sat on the branch of a tree and thought: "That wretched fish was at the root of all my troubles. I have now got rid of it and therefore I am at peace."[1]

Sri Ramakrishna then explained the moral of the story as follows: "The Avadhuta learned this lesson from the kite, that as long as a person has the fish, that is, worldly desires, he must perform actions and consequently suffer from worry, anxiety, and restlessness. When he renounces these desires then his activities fall away and he enjoys peace of the soul."[2]

In the above story, the fish fell from the kite's mouth accidentally and the bird was at peace, finding to its relief and joy that the root cause of its trouble had disappeared. Let us now try to make a slight variation in this story. Let us suppose that our kite is intelligent and has somehow developed the capacity to think deeply. Chased by the battalion of crows and flying helter-skelter, it begins to think:

There is no way I can eat this fish until these crows leave me, and these louts are not going to leave me in peace as long as the fish is with me. It is impossible for me to outstrip such an overwhelming number of them. The only way I can free myself is by letting go of the fish. After all, the fish is not everything. I can easily do without this one. It cannot be the end of the world for me. Why, I can even get a bigger fish later if I try hard enough.

And our intelligent kite, consciously and voluntarily drops the fish. The crows give up the chase and swoop on the falling fish. From his height above, the wise kite looks down and smiles peacefully.

Attachment-Detachment

Now, the parallel between this story and our discussion: The chasing crows symbolize death, the fish, attachment to the world; the kite is you and I. Just as the kite is never sure when and how the crows will catch up with it, we are also never sure when and how death will catch up with us. As long as the fish remained with the kite, the crows did not give up the chase. As long as the attachment to the world remains within us; death is not going to give up chasing us. Once the kite detached itself consciously from the fish, the crows ceased to torment the kite. Similarly, when we detach ourselves consciously from the world, death will cease to torment us. The presence of the crows became irrelevant to the kite when it gave up its claim on the fish. In the same way, the presence of death will become irrelevant to us when we give up our claim on this world.

Something must be said about the word "world" in the above paragraph, to clarify what exactly is intended in the use of phrases such as "attachment to the world," and "detachment from the world."

What *is* this world? Normally we would at once point our finger to everything around us and say, well, *this* is the world! That would not be an accurate answer, however. A student of Vedanta learns to look at everything from the subjective standpoint. He or she says the world is not out *there*, it is right *here*. In the words of Swami Vivekananda, "It is here, I am carrying it all with me. My own body." [3]

Now let us go back to the story of the kite. There were any number of fish in rivers, lakes, and oceans, and there were thousands in the nets of fishermen. But they were not the cause of the kite's problem. The problem-generator was the one fish the kite had fiercely held in its beak. Similarly, our so-called world is not at all the cause of our problem. The real problem-generator is this little bit of the world, called "my body," to which I am desperately clinging. We need everything in the world out *there* only if it is relevant to the world *here*, my own body and mind. Swami Vivekananda's words convey the idea most powerfully:

> The circle of vision has become so narrow, so degraded, so beastly, so like an animal! No one desires anything beyond this body. Oh, the terrible degradation, the terrible misery of it! What little flesh, the five senses, the stomach! *What is the world* but a combination of stomach and sex? Look at millions of men and women—that is what they are living for. Take these away from them and they will find their life empty, meaningless, and intolerable. Such are we. And this is our mind; it is continually hankering for ways to satisfy the hunger of the stomach and sex. All the time this is going on.[4]

The "crows" which symbolize death, or the destruction of my own little world, are going to haunt me as long as I hold on to the "fish," the attachment to my body that produces unending worldly desires. So I begin to reflect, as the kite did in our story: "There is no way I can enjoy perfect peace and fulfillment as long as the fear of death and the uncertainty of my life span are going to haunt me. I cannot prevent the destruction of my body, which is what death really means. This destruction, even the thought of which gives me the jitters, appears terrible because somehow I have begun to feel myself one with the body. My body-consciousness is responsible for the mess I find myself in. Like the kite that let go of the fish, I shall let go of my body-consciousness—and, like the kite became free from the chasing crows, I shall be freed from death."

Letting go of the body-consciousness is, of course, not as easy as letting go of the fish. But, as we have seen, for the kite in the original story, letting go of the fish was not easy either. It shielded the fish from the marauding crows as if its very life depended on it. It was only through an accident that the fish fell down. But in the modified version of our story, the kite, which surely must have been a rare specimen of its tribe, let go of the fish consciously and voluntarily.

The parallel can be drawn to our human situation also. Most of us are like the kite in the original story. Just as the fish was all-important to it, the body—our "little world"—is all important to us. Problems torment us from every side all the time, but we dare not think of anything beyond this little body and its needs. Whether we admit it or not, whether we are conscious of it or not, the truth is that for most of us the whole world revolves around our own body-mind axis. We are afraid to let go of this axis. Who knows, this may hurtle us headlong into the vast, unknown emptiness where we may have nothing to hold onto! That is the unspoken thought and the unexpressed fear.

But the world is never without at least a few, brave explorers who dare to let go their hold on the body-mind axis and jump into the unknown, transcendent vastness that lies beyond. They are like the kite in the modified version. They have learned to think deeply. Floating on the surface of life satisfies them no more. They want to plunge deep within. In the innermost and deepest recesses of their heart they discover the way to overcome death. They realize that they cannot—indeed, no one can—dissociate the body from death; so they do the next best thing. They dissociate *themselves* from the body, and smile—like our kite did—when death comes to claim the unclaimed lump of flesh and bones. That is it! The body—not the Self—is dust and unto dust it has eventually got to return.

The Mystical Birth

What is the body-consciousness of these brave souls replaced by? By Spirit-consciousness or God-consciousness. Their attachment to the body is replaced by the attachment to God. Their attachment to material life is replaced by the attachment to spiritual life. Dying to the world, they begin living in God—this sums up best the lives of all true seekers of the Divine everywhere. St. Simeon the New Theologian (10th century AD) whose copious writings are included in the Philokalia says:

64

A man who has attained the final perfection is dead and yet not dead, but infinitely more alive in God, with whom he lives, for he no longer lives by himself.

Abd al-Quādi al-Jilānī (1078-1166), the great Persian Sufi of Baghdad, explains how to die to the world in order to begin living in God.

Die then to the creatures, by God's leave, and to your passions, by His command, and you will then be worthy to be the dwelling place of the knowledge of God. The sign of your death to the creatures is that you detach yourself from them and do not look for anything from them. The sign that you have died to your passions is that you no longer seek benefit for yourself, or to ward off injury, and you are not concerned about yourself, for you have committed all things unto God. The sign that your will has been merged in the Divine Will is that you seek nothing of yourself or for yourself—God's Will is working in you. Give yourself up into the hands of God, like the ball of the polo-player, who sends it back and forth with his mallet, or like the dead body in the hands of the one who washes it, or like the child in its mother's bosom.

Of Meister Eckhart (1260-1327), the famous German Dominican theologian, it can virtually be said that every page of his works proclaims death. He says, "The soul must put itself to death. The kingdom of God is for none but the thoroughly dead." And again, "One must be dead to see God."

Theologica Germanica, a fourteenth century text said to have been written by a priest of the Teutonic Order, mentions: "If the Creator shall enter in, the creature must depart, of this be assured." Again and again, through different imageries and words, the same message comes across: As long as we do not become blind to the world, we cannot open our eyes to behold God. As long as we do not die to the world, we cannot begin to live in God. We cannot live in Reality until we have died to illusion.

As we said, the "world" or the "illusion" is basically my own body, its needs and desires, and my identification with them all. How do I die to the world? By ceasing to identify myself with my body, I then become, in the words of Rumi, "a dead man walking."

"The dead body resents nothing," said Swami Vivekananda. "Let us make our bodies dead and cease to identify ourselves with them." By dying to the profane world, the seeker gets a mystical birth in the spiritual world.

Living in God

Those who take to monastic life are expected to renounce everything internally and externally. That everything includes, of course, the attachment to the body, that is, to our "little world" that connects us to the "larger world" outside. The monastic has to become "dead" to the world, both inwardly and outwardly. The internal death takes place when the monastic withdraws his or her body-consciousness and replaces it with God-consciousness. In India, this death is symbolized externally by the funeral rites (*śrāddha*) which the monastic performs a day prior to receiving the *sannyāsa* (renunciate) vows. The *sannyāsī* is thenceforth dead to the world. Just as nothing in the world can attract, repel, frighten, lure, agitate, and excite a dead body, so it cannot a true *sannyāsī*. He remains supremely detached, at peace with himself and at peace with the world. His detachment does not mean nonparticipation; he participates wholeheartedly, with total dedication, but without any self-interest and emotional entanglement. He continues to work, usually even more than the so-called "workaholics." But he has no ax to grind, no score to settle, no ambition to prod him on, no duty or obligation to anybody, anywhere, anytime. He works for the good of others as naturally and freely as the sun gives light. The true *sannyāsī* is free because he is dead to the world and has now begun to live in God.

To be able to live in God, the non-monastic spiritual seeker must also "die," but only internally. He or she may also, at some stage, want to perform the *śrāddha* ritual and sever the ties with the world—but this also must be done only mentally. Outwardly, the non-monastic seeker continues to live like all others, interacting with the world to the extent it is unavoidable, but inwardly remaining totally focused on God. This applies also to monastics who are members of a spiritual community.

Sister Consolata (1903-1946), an Italian Capuchin nun, related her own experience: "As regards the community, I try to consider myself as already dead. In this way, everything becomes indifferent to me and I remain at peace."

Peace is, of course, one of the first things we experience when we die to the world. This is, however, only the start of richer treasures that come as we begin to learn the art of living in God. Total fulfillment, freedom, and perfection are attained when our body-consciousness (or "world"-consciousness) is fully and irrevocably replaced by God-consciousness.

"Death" by choice cannot be separated from "life" by choice. At present most of us are dead to God because we have chosen to be alive to the world. If we want to be true seekers of God, our choice must now be reversed. We must now choose to die to the world in order to begin living in God, *and* we must choose to live in God in order to die to the world. We cannot have the one without the other.

FOOTNOTES:

[1] *The Gospel of Sri Ramakrishna*, 324. The story occurs in the eleventh *skandha* of the *Bhāgavatam*.
[2] *Ibid*.
[3] *CW* 4:244.
[4] *CW* 8:118.

X

Self-Realization

by Swami Chinmayananda

It is interesting how, in the history of thought in the Upanishads, the goal of life, which in the beginning was considered to be a state of deathlessness, later became known as the absence of rebirth. At first the anxiety of the seeker was to end the unavoidable and most horrid of all experiences, death. As knowledge increased, through the right evaluation of life, it soon became clear that death had no sting at all for those who understood that it is but one of the different experiences in life. Death can in no way clip off the continuity of existence. The sages came to the conclusion that birth was the beginning of all pain. Therefore, the goal of life, if it were at all possible to achieve, should be the state of no more rebirths.

Estimating the benefits enjoyed by a person of perfection, through the realization of the Self, it is said in the following verse that "Having attained Me, the great souls are no more subject to rebirth."

> *Having attained Me, the great souls* (mahātmas) *do not again take birth, which is the house of pain and is non-eternal, they having reached the highest perfection,* mokṣa. (Gītā VIII:15)

The dream of rebirth and its destinies belongs to the delusory ego, which is nothing but the Self identifying with Its delusory matter envelopments. Electricity conditioned by the bulb is the light. When the bulb breaks, the light that is an effect merges with its cause, the current that is the same everywhere.

Similarly, the Self conditioned by a particular mind and intellect is the ego (*jīvā*) which suffers rebirth, the agonies of imperfection, disease, decay, and death. Once the mind-intellect is transcended, the ego comes to rediscover that it is nothing other than the Self.

One who experiences the Self as his own real Nature, realizes that he never had any relationship at all with the equipment of feeling and understanding. Just as an awakened man has no longer a relationship with his dream wife and children. When thus the ego awakens to the spiritual cognition of the Self, it ends its march through the thorny path of pain and finitude. Such great souls no longer have any need to manifest in the plane of plurality.

In all other states of existence there is the experience of return. Just as sleep is not the end of life, but a refreshing pause between two spans of activity. Similarly, death is not an end, but often only a restful pause in the unmanifested existence between different embodiments. It was already indicated that, even from higher realms of consciousness, ego-centers will have to return to exhaust their unmanifested cravings (*vāsanās*). Birth, we have already been told, is a house of pain and finitude and therefore, complete satisfaction can be reached only when there is no more rebirth, or no return.

Educated students often ask: "Why, after realizing the Self, should there be no return?" Here, in the following verse of the *Muṇḍakopaniṣad,* we have a clear statement explaining the law behind rebirth.

> *Whosoever desires objects, and broods over them, are born again for the fulfillment of those desires. But in the case of a seer whose longings have found their final consummation, who has realized the Self, desires vanish even here in this life itself.* (III, Sec.II:2)

We have already discussed the genesis of action elsewhere. We found that ignorance of our real Nature, which is all-perfect and all-full, generates vague and fantastic desires in us. This ignorance also makes us feel that it is virtually impossible for us to accept our own real Nature. We found that desires are like a hornet's nest of stinging thoughts, and those thoughts express themselves in the outer world as the selfish actions of an individual. The individual ego naturally has to seek conducive fields of activities for the expression of its desire-prompted activities.

The State of Perfection

Self-realization is the ending of every trace of ignorance in us. In the vital moments of experiencing Selfhood, the God-man drops forever his unawareness of his all-perfect Nature, and after that he cannot have any more desires in him. Desirelessness is generally misunderstood as a negative state. Some think of it as a mental coma, into which a person falls when his disappointed desires begin to putrefy themselves. If this were the case, the great masters of wisdom would not have recommended it as the supreme state of perfection.

Desirelessness, with its accompanying state of mental poise, attained by a master is because of his realization of the Self, the state of absolute Bliss. After a complete dinner and plenty of dessert a fully satisfied person will certainly refuse an offer to take another slice of bread. Similarly, total satisfaction comes from experiencing the perfection of the Self. To the master of realization, sense objects are considered as little toys of life when they are compared to the infinite treasure of joy that has already become his. A millionaire will never be tempted to go to a soup kitchen (food line) hoping to get sumptuous food, even in his dream.

Thus, if the Hindu philosophers glorify the state of desirelessness as the end and be all of life, it is because they know a technique that will make us reach a greater state of perfection. And when we look down from there, the flimsy joys of life would look ridiculous, stupid, and childish. To be desireless is certainly a much more glorious state of fulfillment than trying to chase after the changing objects and beings. Our fulfillment lies in knowing that we already have with us all the happiness that we seek. Therefore, when the great masters talk of the state of desirelessness, they mean the state of full and conscious awareness. In this state there are no longer any regrets at not having things that one had previously longed for. Ignorance was the cause for the desires, once the cause is removed, the effect will no longer be there.

In short, according to the texture of our desires we think, and these thoughts ensure that we are born into various situations identifying ourselves with various forms—born, dying, and reborn again. The seer, who has rediscovered his true identity, leaves off all desires. Therefore, for him there is no longer any reason for making his appearance again in the world for gaining or fulfilling any of his unfulfilled desires.

XI

Awareness

by Nisargadatta Maharaj

Questioner: When an ordinary person dies what happens to him?

Maharaj: According to his belief, it happens. As life before death is but imagination, so is life after. The dream continues.

Q: And what about the *jñānī* (the liberated person)?

M: The *jñānī* does not die because he was never born.

Q: He appears so to others.

M: But not to himself. In himself he is free of things—physical and mental.

Q: Still you must know the state of the person who died, at least from your own past lives.

M: Until I met my guru I knew so many things. Now I know nothing, for all knowledge is in my dream only, and therefore not valid. I know myself and I find no life nor death in me, only pure Being—not being this or that, but just Being. But the moment the mind, drawing on its stock of memories, begins to imagine, it fills the space with objects, and time with events.

As I do not know even this birth, how can I know past births? It is the mind that, itself in movement, sees everything moving, and having created time, worries about the past and the future. The entire universe is cradled in consciousness (*mahā tattva*), which arises where there is perfect order and harmony (*mahā sattva*).

As all waves are in the ocean so are all things physical and mental in Awareness. Therefore, Awareness itself is all important, not the content of it. Deepen and broaden your awareness of yourself and all the blessings will flow. You need not seek anything. All will come to you most naturally and effortlessly. The five senses and the four functions of the mind—memory, thought, understanding, and selfhood; the five elements—earth, water, fire, air, and ether; and the two aspects of creation—matter and spirit, are all contained in Awareness.

Experience is Born of Imagination

Q: Yet you must believe in having lived before.

M: The scriptures say so, but I know nothing about it. I know myself as I am. As I appeared, or will appear is not within my experience, it is not that I do not remember. In fact, there is nothing to remember. Reincarnation implies a reincarnating self. There is no such thing. The bundle of memories and hopes, called "I," imagines itself existing everlastingly and creates time to accommodate its false eternity: To *be*, I need no past or future. All experience is born of imagination; I do not imagine, so no birth or death happens to me. Only those who think of themselves as born can think themselves reborn. You are accusing me of having been born—I plead not guilty! All exists in awareness and awareness neither dies nor is reborn. It is the changeless Reality itself.

The entire universe of experience is born with the body and dies with the body; it has its beginning and end in awareness, but awareness knows no beginning, nor end. If you think it over carefully, and brood over it for a long time, you will come to see the light of Awareness in all its clarity, and the world will fade out of your vision. It is like looking at a burning incense stick; you see the stick and the smoke first; when you notice the fiery point, you realize that it has the power to consume mountains of sticks and fill the universe with smoke. Timelessly the Self actualizes itself, without exhausting its infinite possibilities.

In the incense stick metaphor the stick is the body, and the smoke is the mind. As long as the mind is busy with its contortions, it does not perceive its own source. The guru comes and turns your attention to the spark within. By its very nature the mind is turned outward; it always tends to seek for the source of things among the things themselves; to be told to look for the source within, is, in a way, the beginning of a new life.

Awareness takes the place of consciousness; in consciousness there is the "I," who is conscious, while Awareness is undivided; Awareness is aware of Itself. The "I am" is a thought, while Awareness is not a thought; there is no "I am aware" in Awareness. Consciousness is an attribute, while Awareness is not; one can be aware of being conscious, but not conscious of Awareness. God is the totality of consciousness, but Awareness is beyond all—being as well as not being.

Q: I had started with the question about the condition of a person after death. When his body is destroyed, what happens to his consciousness? Does he carry his sense of seeing, hearing, and so on along with him, or does he leave them behind? And, if he loses his senses, what becomes of his consciousness?

M: Senses are mere modes of perception. As the grosser modes disappear, finer states of consciousness emerge.

Q: Is there no transition to Awareness after death?

M: There can be no transition from consciousness to Awareness, for Awareness is not a form of consciousness. Consciousness can only become more subtle and refined and that is what happens after death. As the various vehicles of man die off, the modes of consciousness induced by them also fade away.

Q: Until only unconsciousness remains?

M: Look at yourself talking of unconsciousness as something that comes and goes! Who is there to be conscious of unconsciousness? As long as the window is open, there is sunlight in the room. With the windows shut, the sun remains, but does it see the darkness in the room? Is there anything like darkness to the sun? There is no such thing as unconsciousness, because

unconsciousness is not experienceable. We infer unconsciousness when there is a lapse in memory or communication. If I
stop reacting, you will say that I am unconscious. In reality I
may be most acutely conscious, only unable to communicate or
remember.

View the World Correctly

Q: I am asking a simple question: there are about four bil-
lion people in the world and they are all bound to die. What will
be their condition after death—not physically, but psychologi-
cally? Will their consciousness continue? If it does, in what
form? Do not tell me that I am not asking the right question, or
that you do not know the answer, or that in your world my question is meaningless; the moment you start talking about your
world and my world as different and incompatible, you build a
wall between us. Either we live in one world or your experience
is of no use to us.

M: Of course we live in one world. Only I see it as it is,
while you do not. You see yourself in the world, while I see the
world in myself. To you, you get born and die, while to me, the
world appears and disappears. Our world is real, but your view
of it is not. There is no wall between us, except the one built by
you. There is nothing wrong with the senses, it is your imagination that misleads you. It covers up the world as it is, with what
you imagine it to be—something existing independently of you
and yet closely following your inherited, or acquired patterns.
There is a deep contradiction in your attitude, which you do not
see and which is the cause of sorrow. You cling to the idea that
you were born into a world of pain and sorrow; I know that the
world is a child of love, having its beginning, growth, and fulfillment in love. But I am beyond love even.

Q: If you have created the world out of love, why is it so full
of pain?

M: You are right—from the body's point of view. But you

are not the body. You are the immensity and infinity of Consciousness. Do not assume what is not true and you will see things as I see them. Pain and pleasure, good and bad, right and wrong; these are relative terms and must not be taken absolutely. They are limited and temporary.

Know the Changeless

Q: In the Buddhist tradition, it is said that a *nirvāṇī*, an enlightened Buddha, has the freedom of the universe. He can know and experience for himself all that exists. He can command, interfere with nature, with the chain of causation, change the sequence of events, even undo the past! The world is still with him, but he is free in it.

M: What you describe is God. Of course, where there is a universe, there will also be its counterpart, which is God. But I am beyond both. There was a kingdom in search of a king. They found the right man and made him king. In no way had he changed. He was merely given the title, the rights, and the duties of a king. His nature was not affected, only his actions. Similarly, with the enlightened man; the content of his consciousness undergoes a radical transformation. But he is not misled. He knows the Changeless.

Q: The Changeless cannot be conscious. Consciousness is always of change, the Changeless leaves no trace in consciousness.

M: Yes and no. The paper is not the writing, yet it carries the writing. The ink is not the message, nor is the reader's mind the message—but they all make the message possible.

Q: Does consciousness come down from Reality or is it an attribute of matter?

M: Consciousness as such is the subtle counterpart of matter. Just as inertia (*tamas*) and energy (*rajas*) are attributes of matter, so does harmony (*sattva*) manifest itself as consciousness. You may consider it in a way as a form of very subtle energy. Wherever matter organizes itself into a stable organism, consciousness appears spontaneously. With the destruction of the organism consciousness disappears.

Q: Then what survives?

M: That, of which matter and consciousness are but aspects, which is neither born nor dies.

Q: If it is beyond matter and consciousness, how can it be experienced?

M: It can be known by its effects of both; look for it in beauty and in bliss. But you will understand neither body nor consciousness, unless you go beyond both.

Q: Please tell us squarely: are you conscious, or unconscious?

M: The enlightened (*jñānī*) is neither. But in his enlightenment (*jñāna*) all is contained. Awareness contains every experience. But he who is Aware is beyond every experience. He is beyond awareness itself.

Q: There is the background of experience, call it matter. There is the experiencer, call it mind. What makes the bridge between the two?

M: The very gap between is the bridge. That, which at the one end looks like matter and at the other as mind, is in itself the bridge. Do not separate Reality into mind and body and there will be no need of bridges.

Consciousness arising, the world arises. When you consider the wisdom and the beauty of the world, you call it God. Know the source of it all, which is in yourself, and you will find all your questions answered.

Q: The seer and the seen; are they one or two?

M: There is only seeing: both the seer and the seen are contained in it. Do not create differences where there are none.

Q: I began with the question about the man who died. You said that his experiences will shape themselves according to his expectations and beliefs.

M: Before you were born you expected to live according to

a plan, which you yourself had laid down. Your own will was the backbone of your destiny.

Q: Surely karma interfered.

M: Karma shapes the circumstances; the attitudes are your own. Ultimately your character shapes your life and you alone can shape your character.

Q: How does one shape one's character?

M: By seeing it as it is, and being sincerely sorry. This integral seeing-feeling can work miracles. It is like casting a bronze image; metal alone, or fire alone will not do; nor will the mold be of any use; you have to melt down the metal in the heat of the fire and cast it in the mold.

XII

Overcoming Illusion

by Hazrat Inayat Khan

Is immortality to be gained, or to be acquired? No, it is to be discovered. It is only to make one's vision keen; in other words, to explore oneself, and that is usually the last thing that one does. People enjoy exploring the tomb of Tutankhamen in Egypt, to find mysteries, despite the mystery hidden in their own heart. Tell them about any mystery existing outside themselves, and they are delighted to explore it. But you tell them to see in themselves and they think it is too simple. They think, "I know myself. I am a mortal being. I do not want to die, but death awaits me." They create difficulties, and complexities by their own complex intelligence. They do not like the straight way, they like the zigzag way, they enjoy puzzles. Even if there is a door before them, they say: "No I do not like it." If a door opens before them, they do not wish to come out by that door, they prefer to be in the puzzle. It is a greater joy not to be able to find the door for a long time. One who is thus enjoying the puzzle, is horrified when he sees the door out. The saying of the Prophet is: "Die before death." One need not die. Play it! One should play death and find out what it is. The whole mystical cult is that play, playing death. That play becomes the means by which to understand the mystery hidden behind life.

Man constitutes spirit and matter in himself. What is matter? Crystallized spirit. What is spirit? The original substance. Spirit may be likened to running water, matter to ice. But if there are water and ice, the water will run, the ice will stay where it is. This does not mean that ice does not have to return to its original condition, but its time has not yet come. Therefore, the water will first proceed and the ice will stay where it is. The substance, therefore, stays where it is, but the life, the spirit, passes away. What is necessary, therefore, for a person, is to make the spirit independent of the mortal covering, even if it is for a moment. By that the fear of death naturally vanishes, because then one begins to see the condition after death here on earth. It is this physical cover that has imprisoned, so to speak, the soul in it and the soul finds itself in prison and it cannot see itself, it can only see the cover.

Rumi explains it most beautifully in a poem that he has written on sleep, because it is in sleep that the soul naturally becomes independent of this mortal garb. He says: "Those suffering pain, forget their pain when they are in the arms of sleep. The kings forget their crown and throne. The soul finds itself in that sphere, which is its own and comes back in this prison recuperated."

And the continual longing of the soul is for freedom from this imprisonment. Rumi begins his book, the *Masnavi*, with this lamentation of the soul to free itself. But is it to free the soul by actual death, by a suicide? No, it is not meant like that, mystics have done it. It is by playing death that one arrives at the knowledge of life and death, and it is the secret of life that will make the soul free.

The Process of Playing

The different planes of existence hidden behind the cover of this physical body then begin to manifest to the person who plays dead. All different ways of concentration, of meditation, which are prescribed by the teacher to the pupil, are all that process of playing. They in themselves are nothing. They are a play. What is important is what one finds out as an outcome of that play, what one discovers in the end. Of course, the play begins with self-negation. And a person who likes to say twenty times in the day, "I" does not like to say "I am not, Thou art." But he does not know that this claim of "I" is at the root of all his trouble. It is this claim that makes him feel hurt by a small insult, or by a little disturbance. The amount of pain that this illusion gives him is so great that it is just as well he got rid of it. But that is the last thing he would do. He would give up his last penny, but not the thought of "I". He would hold it as it is the dearest thing to him. This is the entire difficulty and the only hindrance on the path of spiritual perfection.

Very often people ask: "How long has one to go in the spiritual path?" There is no limit to the length of this path, and yet if one is ready, it does not need a long time. It is a moment and one is there. How true it is, what the wise of past ages said to their followers, "Do not go directly in the temple, first walk fifty times around it." The meaning was, "First get a little tired, then enter." Then you value it. One values something for which one makes an effort. If something comes without effort, it is nothing to him. If the government asks a tax for the air which one breathes, people will protest against it. Yet they do not know that there is no comparison between the air and the money they posses. The value of the one is incomparably greater than that of the other. Yet the most valuable things are attained with the least effort, but one does not realize their importance. One would rather have something that is attained with a great effort, and in the end may prove to be nothing.

It is very simple to think: "Why should every being have that innate desire for living, if continual life is impossible?" For there is no desire in the world that does not have its answer. The answer to every desire, is somewhere, the fulfillment of every desire must come one day. Therefore, it is without doubt that this desire of living must be fulfilled. And the fulfillment of this desire is in getting above the illusion that is caused by ignorance of the secret of life.

PART FOUR

Toward
Eternal Life

The happiness of the drop
is to die in the river.

Ghazal of Ghalib

Many of us spend a lot of time looking for philosophies or religions that in some way give us more time. We seek immortality through our belief in reincarnation or in the belief that our existence will continue in a heaven (or even a hell.) But for whom is it that we seek this immortality? Is it for this physical entity? Is it for this collection of vices and virtues? When we think of immortality, is it the notion that in some way this earthly personality will endure endlessly? Some will say, "No, it is not the body or personality that survives. It is the soul." But this is also an individualization which will cease when true unity is. All images and theories are products of a bifurcating mind which depends on duration and constant change in order to manifest its presence.

How then can ordinary mind (time) answer a question on eternity? Zen reaches for a knowing in the now. The practices are designed to help us disengage ourselves from the illusions of ordinary mind. *Satori* or enlightenment provides a knowing of Reality. In Reality (the Timeless), there is no concern with immortality. For Reality is infinite and eternal; it is not dependent on a sequence of events. If I aspire to live forever, I am then denying eternity. Instead of constantly reaching for the next moment, we should know the present, the Now. Then all the illusory aspirations to find immortality will give way to a knowing of the Timeless.

The Upside Down Circle
Zen Master Gilbert

XIII

The Longing for Immortality

by Haridas Chaudhuri

The desire for immortality has been throughout history a powerful motivation of human conduct. It has inspired the noblest and most daring of human deeds. Man has embraced death with a smiling face with a view to conquering death. He has accepted extinction in one form in order to gain imperishable glory in another form. He has sacrificed life evanescent in order to gain life everlasting. The longing for immortality has indeed expressed itself in various ways.

Immortality is essentially an attribute of consciousness. It is an attribute of wisdom, love, and dedication to higher values. By boldly looking death in the face, man overcomes death. By realizing the fundamental truth about life and death, he goes beyond life and death. By perceiving his eternal relationship to the Supreme he participates in the life eternal of the Supreme. By gaining insight into the mystery of time, he is lifted out of the perishing moments of time. By virtue of his identification with higher values and in proportion to his fulfillment of them in life, man appropriates the imperishable property of higher values.

Finally, man attains immortality by achieving integration of personality, and by probing into the nontemporal dimension of his being. A thoroughly integrated person becomes fearless because he discovers his rootedness in the Eternal.

Let us see in what different ways down through the ages man's basic longing for immortality has sought fulfillment.

Social Immortality

First of all, the passion for immortality seeks fulfillment in society. It may assume the form of desire for children—for bright and illustrious children. Through the uninterrupted continuation of progeny, a person gains a sense of immortality. His name is immortalized in the annals of the family tree.

The longing for immortality may also assume the form of leaving some creditable achievement for succeeding generations to admire. Ancient rulers of Egypt used to create pyramids. The great emperor, Sajahan wanted to immortalize his wife by creating the magnificent Taj Mahal. By immortalizing his beloved wife he also secretly desired to immortalize himself. Creative thinkers, poets, painters, and so on, attain immortality by leaving behind them immortal works of artistic creation. Social workers achieve immortality by pouring out their life blood in building some great social institution, such as a school, a hospital, a research institute, a church, and so on. Martyrs gain immortality by giving their lives for a noble cause. Politicians seek immortality through self-identification with the prosperity and the glory of the mother land. Humanitarians identify themselves with the survival, welfare, and progress of the human race.

Idealistic Immortality

The longing for immortality may seek fulfillment through the contemplation and realization of timeless ideas, forms, or values. When that happens, immortality assumes the pure idealistic form.

An artist beholds the enchanting form of beauty in a little flower or in a charming landscape. In contemplating the timeless essence of beauty he feels lifted above the realm of perishable things. He has a feeling of participation in its nontemporal being. His own existence is merged in it, through contemplative oneness. He may feel that now that he is one with the immortal form of beauty, it does not matter if he dies as a particular physical entity.

Similarly, a scientist may be searching for truth in a particular sphere of nature. He has a sense of dedication to truth and identification with truth. Once in a while, he catches a glimpse of the truth he is trying to articulate and establish. By virtue of his vision of truth, he participates in truth's nontemporal being. At the exalted moment of his truth-vision, he experiences immortality. He feels lifted out of the realm of death in the imperishable abode of light and knowledge. His inner being is suffused with the profound joy of communion with truth.

Let us now sum up the foregoing. Social immortality consists in one's feeling of oneness with the society—with its survival, welfare, and progress. By virtue of devotion to a noble social cause, the individual dies to live in the advance of society. Idealistic immortality consists in one's dynamic self-identification with some cultural values, such as scientific pursuit, aesthetic creation, ethical perfection, and so on. It is unitive contemplation of the timeless essence of some great idea.

Personal Immortality

It should, however, be observed here that man's longing for immortality is not completely satisfied in terms of social, cultural or dualistic immortality. The average human being secretly desires for the immortality of his own individual existence as a unique and distinct person. This may be called personal immortality. If the ostensible facts of experience do not lend support to personal immortality, his creative imagination proceeds to fulfill this irrepressible psychic need in sublimated forms.

Broadly speaking, there are two types of people. They are, to use the words of William James, the tough-minded and the tender-minded. The tough-minded people are hard boiled, realistic, and extroverted. They are willing to adjust themselves to the harsh realities of life. They are satisfied with sociocultural immortality, that is, the immortality of some great achievement in social or cultural fields.

But those who are tender-minded secretly wish for the prolongation of their own personal, individualized existence. It is not enough for them to leave at death a legacy of creative action. In order that life may make sense, one must also individually continue to live after death in some form or other. A valuable social or cultural achievement would, for the tender-minded, lose its value if it cannot contribute to the author's prolongation of life beyond the grave. If the facts of actual experience—the facts of common sense, science and self-realization—do not lend support to the idea of indefinite, personal Immortality, the miracle of faith must be invoked to fulfill one's irrepressible psychic need for it.

So, the notion of personal immortality—the indefinite prolongation of the individual after death—plays a dominant role in popular religion and theology. It assumes various forms.

Some visualize personal immortality in terms of bodily resurrection. It is considered possible for the virtuous and the faithful to rise from tombs one day and make a triumphal entry into the supernatural Kingdom of Heaven in order to enjoy the immortal company of the merciful Godhead.

If and when it is realized that the gross physical body is not an indispensable component of an individual human being's spiritual existence, the ideal of disembodied immortality on higher spiritual planes gains prominence. A virtuous and faithful person goes back to the paradise from which he had a fall on account of his sinful defiance of divine authority. He acquires a new celestial body. It is made of subtle, supernatural substance. It enables him to participate in the indescribable glory and supernatural delight of at-one-ment with the Heavenly Father in paradise. Thus, the Christian idea of paradise regained through atonement with the Father in Heaven arises.

The above may be called the supernaturalistic theory of immortality. Supernatural immortality may be static or dynamic. Some people conceive of supernatural immortality in terms of eternal rest and supernal peace in heaven. It is the ecstatic joy of a renewed existence in the kingdom of heaven which is the realm of perfection. But some people—those who are especially ethically-minded—conceive of supernatural immortally in terms of unceasing progress. It is a kind of asymptotic approximation to the infinite goal of perfection. In its upward journey the soul passes through higher and higher levels of consciousness, through the ever-expanding splendors to the Infinite Spirit. Different ideas of supernatural immortality reflect different types of emotional urges of the human psyche. *Vaiṣṇava* supernaturalism in India has elaborately dealt with different types of supernatural self-fulfillment.

Some spiritual seekers wish to dwell in the same lofty plane of existence as that of God (*sālokya*). Some wish to acquire the same form as that of God (*sārupya*). Some wish to acquire the same law of action as that of God (*sādharmya*). Some wish to acquire the same supernatural powers, or the ability to work miracles such as belong to God (*sṛṣṭi*). Some wish to enter into the celestial body of God and get merged in His blissful and universal substance, (*sāyujya*). Some wish to serve God unconditionally (*sevā*), having set aside all personal desires including even the desire for salvation or liberation. The Bengal School of Vaishnavism holds that the spirit of unconditional surrender and service is the loftiest spiritual ideal. Even the notion of salvation appears egotistic when compared with this idea of divine service, regardless of all personal considerations, such as sin and salvation.

But, it should be noted here that behind the willingness to renounce even the desire for liberation, the desire to serve God as a definite individual entity persists. Such a desire to serve God with utmost self-surrender is very commendable as long as one is alive. But when such a desire is projected beyond death, seeking fulfillment in some supernatural realms, the Vedantic criticism that this also is a product of ignorance becomes very pertinent. From the standpoint of supreme wisdom the notions of a personal God, the supernatural region, the desire of personal immortality, even though such personal immortality is visualized in terms of utmost surrender to the Deity—all this belongs in the realm of *māyā*.

The Perfect Devotee

But, the ideal of selfless service of the Supreme here and now in this very world is an element of permanent value in *Vaiṣṇava* mysticism. Let us illustrate this ideal with the aid of an ancient anecdote.

One time the great sage Narada went to have a visit with Lord Krishna in his heavenly abode. On hearing that Krishna had a little headache, Narada was eager to help in whatever way he could. Krishna suggested that a little dust taken from the feet of a perfect devotee might cure him of his headache. Narada thought that such a therapeutic item must be easy enough to obtain. Because, was not the whole world full of Krishna devotees?

He first went to some well-known ascetics and yogis. But all of them were shocked to hear the purpose of Narada's visit. How could they allow a particle of dust from their feet to be applied to the great Lord Krishna's forehead? Would not that amount to a great act of sinfulness on their part? So, they thought that the whole thing was either a big joke, or a devil's trap.

Narada now realized the gravity of the situation and the difficulty of his undertaking. So, he now proceeded to Lord Krishna's wife, Rukmini Devi. But no sooner had she learned of the purpose of Narada's visit than she bit her tongue in shame. The Hindu wife's proper place is at the feet of her lord. How can dust from her feet be applied to the husband's forehead? That would indeed be an unthinkable sin. And a shameless violation of social decorum.

Disappointed and disillusioned, Narada went to Lord Krishna to report the whole matter. Krishna smiled, He then recommended the final solution to the problem. He told Narada to go to the remote and obscure village of Vrindavan and seek the cooperation of His humble devotee, Radha. Traveling a long distance, Narada went to Radha and told her everything. Now, Radha's first reaction was that she was not probably the right kind of devotee who could be of real help to her Lord. Who was she after all, when there were so many world-famous ascetics, yogis, mystics, and philosophers? But Narada assured her that in Krishna's own estimation she was an authentic devotee. At that, Radha was delighted. She said, Narada, take this dust from my feet and go to Krishna's place as fast as you can. He must be relieved of his headache at the earliest opportunity. This may be an act of sinfulness, a violation of ethical code and social decorum on my part. It may cost me my salvation and my place in heaven. But when Krishna is in trouble, nothing matters. The happiness of my Lord is my only concern.

According to the Bengal school of *Vaiṣnavism*, unconditional service of the Lord is the very essence of love and devotion. Love is total self-giving to the Divine. The only concern of love is to be ready to serve the beloved in a spirit of total dedication. Considerations of personal sin and suffering fade into insignificance before the joy of divine service. By virtue of such self-effacing love, the devotee is most intimately united with the Divine after death in the supernatural kingdom of heaven. . . .

The Integral View of Immortality

We are now in a position to state briefly the integral theory of immortality. The integral view is the complete statement and logical culmination of the nondualistic approach of Vedanta.

Immortality is an attribute of enlightened consciousness. All men therefore have the potentiality of immortality by virtue of their consciousness. When the personality of an individual is harmonized and integrated, he attains enlightenment. He gains insight into his existential oneness with the all-encompassing Being. The veil of ignorance and separative consciousness is lifted from his eyes. Feelings of fear and insecurity, anxiety and personal unworthiness, are overcome. There is an enlargement of being and joyful participation in the life of the Infinite. In one word, an individual experiences immortality here and now.

But the experience of participation in the life eternal of the Infinite does not mean self-annihilation in the Infinite. Immortality is an attribute of consciousness, of enlightened existence, not of nonexistence. What is annihilated on the attainment of immortality is not the Self, but the ignorant and separative consciousness of the alienated self. The veil of ignorance torn apart, the individual self can now enter into real and fruitful union with the Eternal. When the finite space enclosed within a house becomes aware of its existential oneness with the infinite space, the house does not get demolished. When a particular wave becomes aware of the fact that it is the ocean itself in an individualized mode, it does not perish as a wave. Similarly, when a human individual becomes aware of his inmost self as it is, namely, as an active center of the one undivided Being, it does not get lost and liquidated. On the contrary, it shines with all the glory of the Supreme Being.

The Goal and End of Life

The true meaning of immortality has often been obscured by the confusion between the goal of life and the end of life. The doctrine of liberation or *mokṣa* in Vedanta has two subtle implications. *Moksa* may mean the highest goal of life, namely, spiritual enlightenment. It may also mean the final end or terminus of an individualized form of existence, its re-absorption in the formless eternity. Confusion between these two meanings of *mokṣa* has often been responsible for much misguided spiritual endeavor.

Higher mysticism rightly affirms that all individualized forms of existence have an end in time. No individualized form has any need to endure for eternity, for instance, for billions of years. Nor is there any sense in that. The doctrine of personal immortality in the sense that a person must be rewarded for his virtue with continued existence for billions of years without end is an illusion of the ignorant mind. It is the sublimated wish-fulfillment of the unconscious psyche. It represents the egotistic desire of the unenlightened. It springs from one's blind attachment to the individualized form of one's being. It is the result of ignorant identification with the body, gross or subtle, physical or psychic. So Vedanta and Buddhism rightly affirm that the individual as a particular existent is bound one day to be reabsorbed into the Infinite, whether conceived as formless Being or as Nonbeing. That is the ultimate chronological end of all life. Not to be able to accept this ultimate end fearlessly and cheerfully is a mark of ignorance and egotism.

But the unfortunate thing is that many spiritual seekers and mystics look upon the ultimate end as also the goal of life. The goal of life is enlightenment, not annihilation in the formless Being. It is Self-realization, not self-liquidation. It is the transformation of the ego, the I-sense, not its total destruction. It is the knowledge of things as they are, not the destruction of the Self as it is. But, on account of the confusion in this respect, some mystics set before themselves the goal of self-annihilation in the Absolute. In consequence, they follow the policy of withdrawal from life and society. They tread the path of slow but sure suicide. They smother the will to live, and unconsciously yield to the dark death-wish slumbering in their psyche.

The most valid spiritual ideal of life is to transform one's whole being into an image of the Divine, and not to get lost in the abyss of the Infinite. When an individual learns to live as an individual, that is, as a unique creative center of the Eternal, he attains living immortality (*jīvanmukti*).

The Four Aspects

It may be said that authentic immortality has four essential aspects. First, immortality implies an individual discovery of the nontemporal dimension of his existence. To discover the nontemporal depth is to experience essential oneness with the Eternal, here and now, while living in the flesh. This may be described as living immortality. It is reflected in the statement "I am in essence one with the Supreme (*Brahman*)."

Secondly, immortality implies conscious union with the Infinite, without loss of personal existence or individuality. It is participation in the life of the Infinite without loss of freedom and personality. The I-sense is not liquidated, but purged of impurities. It bursts through the shell of separative consciousness and experiences itself as a unique and active center of the cosmic whole. Individuality is not lost, but illuminated. Emancipated from the fetters of egocentricity, it becomes cosmocentric. This may be called existential immortality (*sarvātma-bhāva*).

Thirdly, immortality implies intelligent participation in the creative advance of life, not egotistically, with blind attachment and with consequent fear, anxiety, ambition, and impatience, but in a spirit of nonattachment, with creative vision of the future, in harmony with the cosmic purpose of life. Immortality now assumes the form of conscious cooperation with the cosmic force of evolution—with the dynamic world-spirit. There is a sense of deathless continuity in such a spirit of cosmic cooperation. This may be called evolutionary immortality (*sādharmya mukti*).

Finally, the concept of immortality implies a harmonization of the entire personality and a transformation of the physical organism as an effective channel of expression of higher values. This may be called material immortality (*rupāntar mukti*).

There are some mystics and spiritual seekers who strengthen and purify their bodies just enough to be able to experience the thrilling touch of the Divine. They use the body as a ladder, by climbing which the pure spiritual level—the domain of immortality—is to be reached. On attaining that level, the body is felt as a burden, as a prison house, as a string of chains that holds one in bondage. Dissociation from this last burden of the body is considered a *sine que non* for complete liberation. Continued association with the body is believed to be the result of the last lingering trace of ignorance (*avidyā leśa*). When the residual trace of ignorance is gone, the spirit is finally set free from the shackles of the body.

The above view is based upon a subtle misconception about the purpose of life and the significance of the body. The body is not only a ladder that leads to the realm of immortality, but also an excellent instrument for expressing the glory of immortality in life and society. It is capable of being thoroughly penetrated by the light of the spirit. It is capable of being transformed into what has been called the "Diamond Body." As a result of such transformation, the body does not appear any more to be a burden upon the liberated self. On the contrary, it becomes a perfect image of the Self. It shines as the Spirit made flesh. It functions as a very effective instrument for creative action and realization of higher values in the world. It is purged of all inner tension and conflict. It is liberated from the anxiety of repressed wishes. It is also liberated from the dangerous grip of the death impulse born of self-repression. Mystics who look upon the body as a burden suffer from the anxiety of self-repression and the allurement of the death wish.

Material immortality means decisive victory over both of these demons. It conquers the latent death instinct in man, and fortifies the will to live as long as necessary, as a channel of expression of the Divine. It also liquidates all forms of self-suppression and self-torture, and self-mutilation. As a result the total being of an individual becomes strong and steady, whole and healthy. There is a free flow of psychic energy. It is increasingly channeled into ways of meaningful self-expression. Under the guidance of the indwelling light of the Eternal, it procures increasing manifestation of the spirit in matter.

XIV

The Gift of Immortality

by Eknath Easwaran

[*This article is taken from* Dialogue with Death, *Sri Eknath's commentary on the* Kaṭha Upaniṣad. *It contains a dialogue between a young seeker, Nachiketa, and his teacher, Lord Yama, the King of Death.*]

Modern civilization believes that the purpose of the body is to enjoy pleasure. Hindu and Buddhist mystics put it very differently: because of our desires for pleasure and profit we take on a body over and over again, life after life, through millions of years of evolution. Against the vast backdrop of reincarnation there is no hit and miss in this; it is all precisely governed by the law of karma. As long as personal desires continue, the body will continue; and as long as the body continues, death will continue. When we cease to think of ourselves as separate creatures with separate, personal needs, we break through identification with the body and conquer death—not in some other world, some afterlife, but here and now. Lord Yama tells Nachiketa,

> When all desires that surge in the heart
> Are renounced, the mortal becomes immortal.
> When all the knots that strangle the heart
> Are loosened, the mortal becomes immortal.
> This sums up the teachings of the scriptures.

This is the purpose of life, the culmination of the long journey of evolution. On the physical level, the human body at one end of this journey and a bacterium at the other differ only in degree. If you put a little sugar in their environment, I once read, bacteria will move toward it; put in something they do not like and they will move away. I thought to myself, "How human!" That is the nature of life on the physical level, and there is not much freedom in it. Only the human being has the capacity to defy the conditioning of pleasure and choose not to identify with the body but with the changeless, eternal Self. In this sense, only a few of us—men and woman like Francis of Assisi, Teresa of Avila, Thérèse of Lisieux, Sri Ramakrishna—can accurately claim the title of *homo sapiens*. The rest of us, though we are dressed for the part, have not yet come into the glory of our inheritance.

As long as we identify with the body we are fragments, occupying a limited portion of space and perhaps eighty years in time. But there is a much vaster "I," the Self, compared with which this tiny ego-corner is no more nor less than a prison. Our whole modern way of life is based on the belief that we can enjoy ourselves in this prison, find fulfillment in this prison, leave our mark on posterity in this prison, all because we have leave to walk about for a while in the prison yard and perhaps play a little volleyball. If we could only see how narrow this life is, how petty, how quickly ended, we would concentrate all our effort on escaping from it once and for all.

During the second part of life we learn to defy all the selfish desires that human existence is prey to, hundreds of them, through the practice of meditation and the allied disciplines. This is not negating desires; it is unifying them—transforming them from selfish to selfless, from individual to universal. This unification of desires leads to the integration of personality in its full glory. Instead of living just for one person, we live for the welfare of all, for the happiness of all. The partitions of the ego are down. We live in all creatures, which means we live a thousandfold more. Everything is magnified: our sympathy, our sensitivity, our strength, our love, our capacity to give and help and serve. This is not the extinction of personality; it is its perfection. As Saint Francis de Sales puts it, the individual personality merges in the divine, as the light of a star when the sun arises "is ravished into and absorbed in the sun's sovereign light, within which it is happily mingled and allied."

This does not mean that the body is lost. The body remains, but we no longer identify ourselves with it. Physical conditioning has no more sway over us, so we are free to give the body the very best of care: good, nourishing food, plenty of vigorous exercise, adequate rest and recreation. And the body responds with health, resilience, and an inner glow of beauty. The tremendous motivation to contribute to the welfare of the whole world releases vitality for a long, vigorous, victorious life, in which all our deepest desires are fulfilled.

The usual idea is that this is a dull, drab, desireless existence. Just the opposite. It is the man or woman who has mastered desires who really enjoys the innocent pleasures of life. To give a small example, I eat excellent, nutritious food, go to concerts, take every opportunity to see a good play or a tasteful film. When I go to the beach for a long, fast walk, usually taking a few friends and dogs along for company, my mind and body enjoy the exercise and the soothing music of the surf the way a child enjoys ice cream. All these are part of my *sādhanā*, for they enable my body and mind to function smoothly for many years of hard, sustained, selfless work.

Equal Love For All

When all desires are right desires, says the *Theologica Germanica*, "All things are lawful, save one tree and the fruits thereof . . . that is, self-will." Saint Augustine puts it even more simply: "Love; then do as you will." This word *love* is used so commonly today that we have all but forgotten what it means.

Because of our physical orientation, we think in terms of one-to-one relationships over candlelight and wine, "dancing cheek to cheek," or sitting together under a swaying palm tree admiring a Caribbean moon. All this is just the shadow of love. We are not made to love only one or two individuals. We have the immense capacity to be in love with everyone, with every creature—not in some abstract way, but as the Buddha says, as a mother loves her only child. It is not that we love our partner or children any less. We love them much more, but now we feel equal love for all.

There is nothing sentimental about this. It is thoroughly practical. Every child becomes your child, each creature part of your family; you take care of the planet just as you would your home. Which of us would eat up all the food in the house, burn the back porch for firewood, dump garbage in the bathtub, spray the rooms with noxious chemicals, and then tell our children, "Whatever is left is yours?" Similarly, those who are in love with creation lead a simple, self-reliant life as trustees of the world's resources, returning to life much more than they take away.

Such a person has really ceased to be an individual. He or she is a lasting beneficial force, whose power to improve the lives of others is in no way diminished when the physical body is shed at the time of death. Saint Francis, to take just one example, cannot be described in the terms of a police report: five foot four, one hundred and twenty pounds, living for forty-three years. That is the container; Francis is a force affecting our lives today exactly as it did when it was embodied in Assisi. As Yama would put it, though his body may have been in a cave in Umbria, the Self in him could move the hearts and change the lives of men and woman all over Europe. Where is the difference between then and now? He is separated from us in time instead of space, but that is all. I feel sure that Francis's guidance is as real to some people today as it was to Brother Giles and Brother Leo—and perhaps more real than some of the realities of everyday life that we take for granted.

Or look at a figure much closer to us in time, whom I have seen and heard and walked with, Mahatma Gandhi. Even though he laid down his life more than thirty years ago, the force of nonviolence Gandhi embodied is still at work among us, inspiring us and reassuring us that we do have the capacity to meet the worldwide threat of destruction—not by the love of power, as nations try to do, but by the power of love. The first is the power to destroy; power that is invincible is the power to support and serve.

Only with men and women of this stature do we get a proper measure for our own lives. There is a million times more joy in living for all than in satisfying personal urges, however pleasant. Many, many people, if they could be granted their heart's desire, would say, "I want to retire to the Riviera and really live it up. I want to live on Molokai with the film star of my dreams. I want to play golf all week long, speak French like a native, see the pyramids, complete my collection of antique dolls, and see my face on the cover of *Time* as Woman of the Year." Yama would shake his head: "You are meant for a million times more."

Unifying Desires

When all our urges merge in the tremendous desire for Self-realization, the fulfillment of that desire floods our hearts with joy. "Take the happiness of a man whose worldly desires are satisfied," the Upanishads tell us, "Let that be one measure of joy. Millions of times greater is the joy that comes when all selfish desires are stilled."

"There is no greater gift than this," Nachiketa tells the King of Death, "and I can have no better teacher than You." In the Hindu tradition, it is said that the Lord is extending the gift of immortality to each of us. But we are holding a few pennies in our hands. I do not know if you have seen infants in this dilemma; it happens at a particular stage of development, when they have learned to grasp but not quite mastered letting go.

They have a rattle in one hand, you offer them a toothbrush, and for a while they just look back and forth at the toothbrush, then the rattle, then the toothbrush again. You can almost see the gray matter working: "I want that toothbrush, but how can I take it? My hand is already full."

Similarly, I think, all of us ask for a long while, "What is this gift? How do I know it is real? Give it to me first; then I will let the pennies go." The Lord only smiles and waits. He can offer the gift, but for us to take it, we have to open our hands. And there comes a time when we want something more than pennies so passionately that we no longer care what it costs. Then we open our hands, and discover that for the pennies we have dropped, we have received an incomparable treasure.

This is never easy. Everyone finds it difficult to let go. The whole question is, how much do we want something more, something that time cannot take away? In my own case, I can testify that I too once took a good deal of pleasure in certain private pastimes, which after all caused no one any harm. When I began to see that to unify my desires I would have to detach myself from these pastimes, for a long time I did not think I would be able to do it. My intellect kept asking, "Is this really necessary? Even if you succeed, won't it be a woeful loss?" I began to let go in earnest the day I realized that no matter what satisfactions I attained, Yama was waiting down the road, ready to take them away. After that, the conquest of death came first, last, and in between; everything else was a distraction. Now nothing is a distraction. I enjoy everything much more than before, for now every facet of my life serves one overriding goal. I have not lost anything; I have only gained.

We are talking here about overcoming death. That is the stake for which we are playing. Petty stakes like pleasure and profit cannot be mentioned in the same breath. And the game is not open for long. The croupier is standing by the tables saying as they do in Monte Carlo, "*Faites vos jeux*! Ladies and gentlemen, place your bets." The wheel spins, hopes rise and fall, and the round is over; Yama reaches out and rakes the counters in. Life is too short to play for nickels and dimes; we are meant to break the bank. . . .

The Other Shore

When you break through the surface of awareness in meditation, you may feel as if you have cast adrift in a shoreless, seething sea—the sea of change, the ocean of birth and death. Only after years of inward traveling, when the senses are closed to the outside world and you are miles deep in consciousness, do you catch sight of a farther shore, beyond change, beyond separateness, beyond death. Suddenly, when the mind is still, the words of the *Gītā* on which you are meditating open up and take you in, and the sound of them reverberates through consciousness as if you have found the pitch to which every cell vibrates:

> You were never born; how can you die?
> You have never suffered change; how can you be changed?
> Unborn, eternal, immutable, immemorial,
> You do not die when the body dies.

When this happens, no matter what the rest of the world may say, you know for certain that you have been born into this sea for no other purpose than to reach its other shore, which is our real home.

Not long ago, walking on the beach one morning after a storm, I was surprised to find the sand littered with creatures not much bigger than an old-fashioned silver dollar. They are called, I am told, *velellas*, "little sailors," for they have a disk-like body that floats on the sea and an upright fin that catches the wind. They go where the wind and currents carry them; they have no other power of motion. And the sail is set; they have no choice of direction. Halfway in evolution between organism and colony, they have no fixed life span. They might have drifted on the ocean for years, with no reason to care which direction they were carried in, until a California squall swept them by the thousand onto the nearest shore. In the water, I thought, they must look beautiful, a miniature blue armada with translucent sails scudding before the wind. Now their fragile bodies covered the beach, and whether they were jellyfish or floating colonies or some even lower order; they had passed from this life.

"So many! I had not thought death had undone so many." Even with such simple creatures the theater of death opens for me. The beach seemed like an Elizabethan stage, where a tragedy is not considered complete until the boards are covered with bodies. But in this drama there was no antagonist. I could not blame the sea; its nature is to move. I could not blame the wind; the winds of change have to blow. And there was no question about their direction: all creatures have the same destination; all are going to the same land. But I thought to myself, "If only they had been able to set that sail!" They could have sailed in the teeth of the wind—against the current of life, as the Buddha says, all the way to a farther shore.

It is our blessing as human beings to have sails that we can set as we choose. No other creature has this capacity; it is our precious legacy. And two great saints from East and West, Sri Ramakrishna and Saint Francis de Sales, encourage us with almost identical words: "Set your sail for the other shore." The wind is blowing; we have no choice but to move. But we have a sail that can be set, and we have testimonies like the *Katha Upaniṣad* to give us the goal, the direction, and the charts. The rest is up to us.

Today I went to a hospital. As I walked down the corridors, people were dying—not just the old but the young as well. Some of them might have been born here a few years before; soon their bodies would expire here. How quickly it all passes! Time, Shankara says, is a wheel with three hundred and sixty-five spokes, rolling down our lives. We may run fast or slow, but every body is overtaken by that wheel.

The friend I had come to see was dying of lung cancer. I sat beside her silently, holding her hand and repeating my mantra in my mind, until her body gave up and ceased struggling to breathe. Within a short while it was over. As I walked back along the long corridors, it seemed to me that I was seeing the same scenes that launched the Buddha on his search for the Eternal twenty-five hundred years before. There was disease, of course. There was old age, decrepitude, decay, and there was death, waiting for us all.

I wanted a long, fast walk. Across the street was a vast new shopping center, with covered arcades that offered protection from the summer sun. Inside I saw hundreds of people, old and young, wandering from window to window—looking at things, calculating, longing, buying, unmindful of what was happening on the other side of the street. How easily we can be bought! Nachiketa was offered the fulfillment of all worldly desires; our lives can be purchased with foot-long candy bars, stuffed toys, decorated T-shirts, and video games.

In my grandmother's language, I spent an afternoon with Yama today. He stood in that hospital at the end of a long, long corridor, waiting. Many of those in the hospital beds would reach him soon. The staff, the visitors, the shoppers across the street, probably had farther to go. But in time, everyone had to go down that corridor and meet Death. And there was nothing threatening in his face. "I carry out my function," he seemed to say. "If you choose, you can pass me by."

To me, this is a very personal message. The gift of immortality is not the birthright of just one or two. There is something of Nachiketa in all of us; that is the glory of our human heritage. So his story concludes with a blessing intended for us all:

Nachiketa learned from the King of Death
The whole discipline of meditation.
Freeing himself from all separateness,
He won immortality in the Self.
So blessed is everyone who knows the Self!

May each of us realize that blessing, and live in that presence within us which death can never touch!

Pronunciation of Sanskrit Letters

a (b*u*t)	k (s*k*ate)	ḍ ˌno	m (*m*uch)
ā (mom)	kh(*K*ate)	ḍh⎱English	y (*y*oung)
i (*i*t)	g (*g*ate)	ṇ ⎰equiva-	r (d*r*ama)
ī (b*ee*t)	gh(*g*awk)	lent	l (*l*uck)
u (s*u*ture)	ṅ (si*ng*)	t (*t*ell)	v (*w*ile/*v*ile)
ū (p*oo*l)	c (*ch*unk)	th (*t*ime)	s (*sh*ove)
ṛ (ri*g*)	ch(mat*ch*)	d (*d*uck)	ṣ (bu*sh*el)
ṝ (rrr*ri*g)	j (*J*ohn)	dh (*d*umb)	s (*s*o)
ḷ no	jh (*j*am)	n (*n*umb)	h (*h*um)
English	ñ (bu*n*ch)	p (s*p*in)	ṁ (nasaliza-
equiva-	ṭ ˌno	ph (*p*in)	tion of
lent	ṭh⎱English	b (*b*un)	preceding
e (pl*a*y)	⎰equiva-	bh (ru*b*)	vowel)
ai (h*i*gh)	lent		ḥ (aspira-
o (t*o*e)			tion of
au(c*ow*)			preceding
			vowel)

MANANAM BACK ISSUES
(continued from page ii)

For information contact:
Chinmaya Mission West
P.O. Box 129
Piercy, CA 95587
(707) 247-3488